Main Findings from the 2020 Risks that Matter Survey

This work is published under the responsibility of the Secretary-General of the OECD. The opinions expressed and arguments employed herein do not necessarily reflect the official views of OECD member countries.

This document, as well as any data and map included herein, are without prejudice to the status of or sovereignty over any territory, to the delimitation of international frontiers and boundaries and to the name of any territory, city or area.

The statistical data for Israel are supplied by and under the responsibility of the relevant Israeli authorities. The use of such data by the OECD is without prejudice to the status of the Golan Heights, East Jerusalem and Israeli settlements in the West Bank under the terms of international law.

Note by Turkey

The information in this document with reference to "Cyprus" relates to the southern part of the Island. There is no single authority representing both Turkish and Greek Cypriot people on the Island. Turkey recognises the Turkish Republic of Northern Cyprus (TRNC). Until a lasting and equitable solution is found within the context of the United Nations, Turkey shall preserve its position concerning the "Cyprus issue".

Note by all the European Union Member States of the OECD and the European Union

The Republic of Cyprus is recognised by all members of the United Nations with the exception of Turkey. The information in this document relates to the area under the effective control of the Government of the Republic of Cyprus.

Please cite this publication as:
OECD (2021), *Main Findings from the 2020 Risks that Matter Survey*, OECD Publishing, Paris, https://doi.org/10.1787/b9e85cf5-en.

ISBN 978-92-64-35607-8 (print)
ISBN 978-92-64-94885-3 (pdf)

Cover photo credit: © Artem Oleshko/Shutterstock.com.

Corrigenda to publications may be found on line at: www.oecd.org/about/publishing/corrigenda.htm.

© OECD 2021

The use of this work, whether digital or print, is governed by the Terms and Conditions to be found at http://www.oecd.org/termsandconditions.

Contents

Foreword 6
Acknowledgements 7
Editorial 9
Executive summary 11

1. Taking the pulse of OECD countries 13

   1.1. Staying healthy and paying the bills: Unpacking short-term risk perceptions

   1.2. Retirement, health and long-term care dominate long-term perspectives

   1.3. Risk perceptions are well founded

2. Is social protection working? 29

   2.1. A social contract for a pandemic

   2.2. Low public confidence in income support

   2.3. Mixed perceptions of public programme effectiveness

   2.4. Whose programme is this? Public opinion about programme design

3. Calls for greater social protection - if the price is right 41

   3.1. Support for a government safety net remains high throughout the OECD

   3.2. Putting a price tag on social security

   3.3. How to fund social programmes? Redistributive preferences in a pandemic

References 50
Annex A. Occurrence of financial difficulties during COVID-19 51
Notes 52

Foreword

The OECD Risks that Matter programme is a key output of the 2018 OECD Social Policy Ministerial in Montréal, Canada. Ministers called on the OECD to help governments better incorporate citizens' opinions in the policy making process, better understand both real and perceived risks people face, and better adapt social protection to a world characterised by rapidly changing risks and opportunities. These priorities were outlined in the Social Policy Ministerial Statement, entitled "Social Policy for Shared Prosperity: Embracing the Future" (https://www.oecd.org/social/ministerial/).

In line with these goals, the OECD launched the first Risks that Matter (RTM) survey in spring 2018 under the supervision of the OECD's Employment, Labour and Social Affairs Committee. Results from RTM 2018 showed that people in even the wealthiest countries in the world were clearly worried about their health and economic security, and they wanted government to do more when providing social protection.

Informed by these findings, the Secretariat began planning the 2020 round of RTM with a focus on economic insecurity and incorporating citizen feedback in policy design. But when COVID-19 struck, the focus shifted to better capture people's experiences during the pandemic.

In autumn 2020, RTM 2020 survey asked 25 000 respondents across 25 OECD countries about their experiences during the pandemic, their risk perceptions, and their preferences for government action. A first brief drawing on RTM 2020 data, entitled "The Long Reach of COVID-19" (OECD, 2021[1]), was published in spring 2021, focusing on households' economic insecurity. The current report presents broader results – on general risk perceptions and preferences for government policies – from the RTM 2020 survey.

The COVID-19 crisis has created an urgent need to put in place smart and holistic social policy responses to address the challenges people have been facing. With this urgency in mind, this report situates risk perceptions and social policy preferences in the context of the pandemic. The OECD finds that respondents are very worried about their health, economic security, and long-term care. People who suffered job disruption during the pandemic, youths, and women are particularly stressed. And across OECD countries, respondents are critical about the degree of government support they receive. Most are calling for greater government intervention to ensure social protection.

As the economic recovery takes shape, governments must better incorporate citizen feedback in programme design and reform – to ensure inclusive and sustainable growth that benefits everyone.

Acknowledgements

This report was written by Valerie Frey, under the supervision of Monika Queisser, Senior Counsellor and Head of Social Policy at the OECD; Mark Pearson, Deputy Director of the OECD Directorate for Employment, Labour and Social Affairs; and Stefano Scarpetta, Director of the OECD Directorate for Employment, Labour and Social Affairs.

Adriana Rakshana, Chris Clarke, and Maxime Ladaique provided valuable statistical support at various stages of data collection and analysis. Liv Gudmundson led the publication process and layout design. Fatima Perez and Alastair Wood were also instrumental in publication and dissemination.

The report benefitted from useful feedback from Delegates to the OECD Working Party on Social Policy and the OECD Employment, Labour and Social Affairs Committee, as well as Emanuele Ciani, Sarah Kups, Veerle Miranda and Marissa Plouin of the OECD.

The project was financially supported by member countries' voluntary contributions. Academic researchers at the University of Konstanz (Marius Busemeyer, Sebastian Koos and Florian Kunze) and the University of Lausanne (Carlo Knotz, Mia Gandenberger, Maude Lavanchy, Giuliano Bonoli, Flavia Fossati, Rafael Lalive, Joël Wagner and the Center Enterprise 4 Society) provided constructive feedback on questionnaire content and design and financially supported subsections of the survey. On the part of the University of Konstanz team, financial support from the Cluster of Excellence "The Politics of Inequality" (Deutsche Forschungsgemeinschaft (DFG) Grant No. EXC 2035/1) is gratefully acknowledged.

Editorial

It would be an understatement to say that 2020 was a transformative year.

Hundreds of millions of people around the world suffered the physical and mental health consequences of COVID-19. By the end of June 2021, more than 3.9 million lives had ended because of it. National health systems have been stretched to their limits through several waves of COVID-19 infections.

The health pandemic led to another crisis: that of economic insecurity. Entire economies transitioned to low power mode during national and regional lockdowns, in an effort to slow the transmission of the illness. In turn, the global economy slowed to a crawl. When accounting for both the stark drop in employment and the reduction in hours worked by people who remained in the labour market, COVID-19's negative impact on total hours worked in spring 2020 was ten times greater than that experienced in the first few months of the 2008 global financial crisis (OECD, 2020[2]). By March 2021, hours worked were still 7% below their level in December 2019[1] (OECD, 2021[3]). OECD countries may not recover to pre-pandemic employment levels before 2023, despite the projected rebound in economic activity in 2021 and 2022.

Everyone has been affected. Young adults and low-skill workers were especially hard hit by job disruptions, either in the form of reduced work hours or outright job losses (OECD, 2021[3]). Income losses were widespread. Many people who were able to keep their jobs suddenly found themselves on the "front line" of the pandemic due to their work in essential service sectors. Other workers were thrust into a future of indefinite telework, often while simultaneously caregiving for children who could no longer attend daycare or school in-person.

OECD governments responded to the unprecedented health, economic and social challenges of the pandemic with a range of bold policy measures (OECD, 2020[4]; 2020[5]; 2020[6]; ISSA, 2021[7]). Although expenditure data are still incoming across countries, it is very likely that 2020 will represent the largest expansion of OECD welfare states since the World War II recovery period – and yet people are still falling through the cracks.

It is against this backdrop of upheaval that the second wave of the OECD Risks that Matter survey went into the field in 25 countries in autumn 2020.

This report presents main findings from RTM 2020, and the results paint a stark picture. Responses to the RTM 2020 survey illustrate widespread economic disruption during the pandemic, heightened worries about health and financial security, and, in many cases, calls for greater government intervention in social insurance – even at the cost of higher taxes. The survey thus provides a strong call for bold investment in social protection, not only to ensure a full recovery for everyone, but also to address the structural gaps in access and quality of services that the crisis has once more brought to the fore.

The good news is that many countries are committing massive resources to the recovery. It is crucial that these recovery plans support the reforms needed to close gaps in social protection.

Stefano Scarpetta

Director of Employment, Labour and Social Affairs, OECD

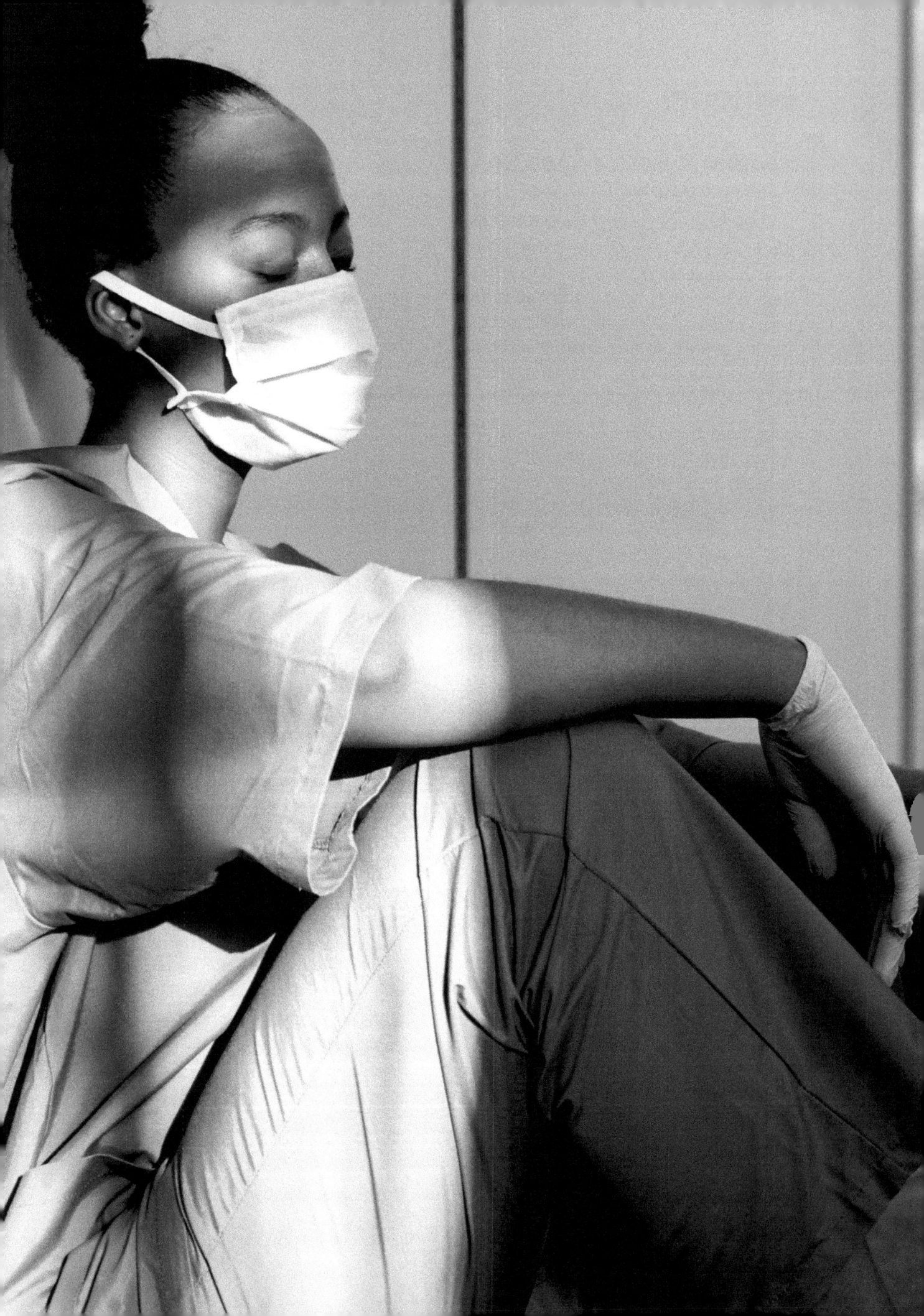

Executive summary

The OECD's 2020 Risks that Matter (RTM) survey takes the pulse of economic health and social security in 25 OECD countries. Carried out in the midst of the pandemic, RTM asks about people's risk perceptions, explores how satisfied they are with their government's social protection, and asks whether – and how – people think public policies in OECD countries should better ensure their social and economic security. These findings offer crucial insights for policy makers trying to improve social protection systems as countries recover from the pandemic.

Key findings

- Looking ahead to 2022, two-thirds of respondents to the 2020 Risks that Matter (RTM) survey say that they are somewhat or very concerned about their household's finances and overall social and economic well-being. When looking only at respondents whose household reported a job loss during the pandemic, the share that is concerned about economic well-being rises to 80.6%, on average across countries. Women tend to be more worried about household finances than men.

- The concerns reflect deep levels of economic insecurity. Nearly half (44.2%) of households, cross-nationally, experienced some form of job disruption during the pandemic, and 11.8% of respondents report that either they or a household member lost a job outright or lost their own business since the start of the crisis. In turn, about one-third of respondents have faced financial difficulties such as having trouble paying a bill or needing to borrow money.

- In the short run, the top perceived risks are falling ill and making ends meet. The top perceived risks in the long run – that is, beyond the next decade – are falling ill, financial security in old age, and securing good-quality and affordable long-term care (both for the respondent and for elderly family members). More than half of all respondents identify these as issues they are concerned or very concerned about.

- Despite the tremendous expansion of social spending in OECD countries during the COVID-19 pandemic, people are sceptical that their government would help them get through financial troubles. Nearly six out of ten respondents say that they have little or no confidence that cash benefits and services provided by their government would sufficiently support them if they were to experience financial difficulties. Most people instead count on personal networks of family and friends.

- Governments are perceived as more effective in some policy areas than others. On average across countries, people are most satisfied with public services around education, health care, and public safety.

- People in OECD countries feel disconnected from programme design and benefit distribution. Only one in five respondents, cross-nationally, feel that their government incorporates their views. And only about one-quarter of respondents say that they get their fair share of benefits relative to the taxes and social contributions they pay.

- Despite these concerns, support for a government safety net remains high throughout the OECD. On average, more than two-thirds (67.7%) of all respondents say they think government should be doing more to ensure their economic and social security.

- When considering the taxes they might have to pay and the benefits they might receive, seven out of ten respondents across countries say that they would support greater spending on public health services – the most popular issue area. Pensions and long-term care are the other areas where people are most willing to invest more in taxes.

1. Taking the pulse of OECD countries

"Health care services for anything other than COVID-19 have been virtually non-existent [in 2020]. Pregnancy, newborn and pre existing health problems have all had treatment cancelled or deferred."

– 33-year-old woman, Ireland

The COVID-19 pandemic heightened health risks and resulted in widespread job losses, reductions in work hours, and significant income drops as countries went into prolonged economic shutdowns to limit the spread of the virus (OECD, 2020[2], 2021[3], 2021[1]). How are people in OECD countries assessing these risks? What issues are weighing most heavily on people's minds?

1.1. Staying healthy and paying the bills: Unpacking short-term risk perceptions

Despite living in some of the wealthiest countries in the world, and with some of the best-developed social protection systems in the world, RTM 2020 respondents feel unsettled about their household's overall social and economic well-being as they look ahead to 2022.

On average across countries, 66.5% of respondents say they are somewhat or very concerned about their household's finances and overall social and economic well-being over the next year or two (Figure 1.1). When looking only at individuals whose household reported a job loss during the pandemic (detailed further in Section 1.3), the share of respondents who are somewhat or very concerned about the next two years rises to 80.6%, on average across countries.

Respondents in northern European countries tend to have the highest levels of confidence about their finances, perhaps reflecting long-standing confidence in their national economies, governments and social protection systems. These attitudes may also reflect expansions in social safety nets during the pandemic, as job retention schemes were widely used and governments invested heavily in family, housing, and unemployment support. Yet even in these more optimistic countries, there is a high degree of concern among people whose household experienced job loss.

Women also report feeling more insecure about their household's finances than men do. This result holds in every country in the sample. On average across countries, women are 5.9 percentage points more likely than men to say that they are concerned or very concerned about their household's finances and economic and social security. These gender gaps are widest in Turkey, Lithuania and Slovenia, where the difference between men's and women's perceptions are around 10 percentage points (Figure 1.2).

It is worth noting this survey presents perspectives from one of the more optimistic moments in the crisis. Risks that Matter ran in 25 countries in September and early October 2020, when most countries were between waves of infection and health and economic data were improving. The third quarter OECD area employment rate was 66.7% – an improvement on the second quarter, when employment had dropped to 64.8%, but still well below 2020's

Figure 1.1. Two-thirds are concerned about their finances and social and economic well-being

Percent of respondents who are "somewhat" or "very" concerned about their household's finances and overall social and economic well-being over the next year or two, by reported experience of job loss in the household since the start of the COVID-19 pandemic, 2020

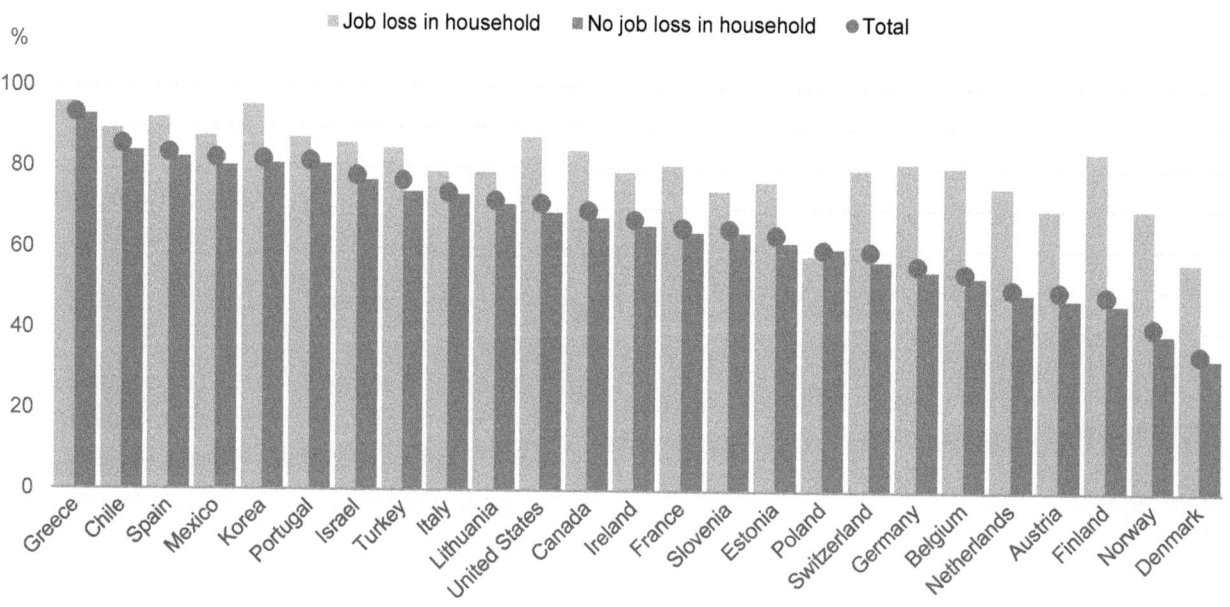

Note: Respondents were asked how concerned they were about their household's finances and overall social and economic well-being in the near future, defined as the next year or two. The response options were "not at all concerned", "not so concerned", "somewhat concerned" and "very concerned". Respondents could also choose "can't choose" as a response option. "Somewhat concerned" and "very concerned" answer choices are aggregated here "Job loss in household" refers to respondents reporting that either they or any member of their household have/has either "Lost their job or been laid off permanently by their employer" and/or "Lost their self-employed job or their own business", since the start of the COVID-19 pandemic.
Source: OECD Secretariat estimates based on the OECD Risks That Matter 2020 survey, https://www.oecd.org/social/risks-that-matter.htm.

Figure 1.2. Women are more concerned about household economic insecurity in every country

Percent of respondents who are "somewhat" or "very" concerned about their household's finances and overall social and economic well-being over the next year or two, by gender, 2020

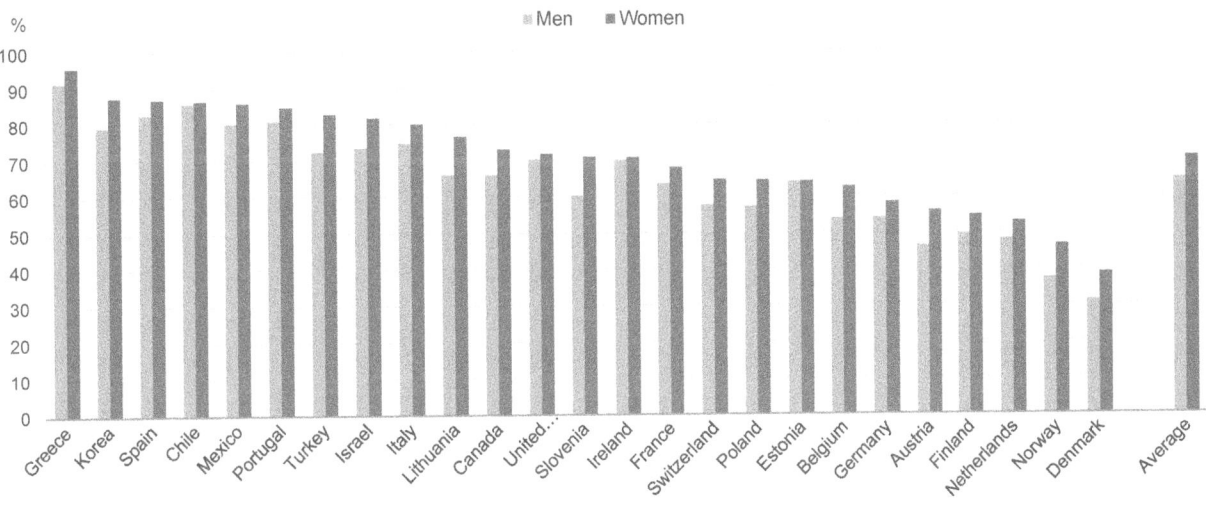

Note: Respondents were asked how concerned they were about their household's finances and overall social and economic well-being in the near future, defined as the next year or two. The response options were "not at all concerned", "not so concerned", "somewhat concerned" and "very concerned". "Somewhat concerned" and "very concerned" answer choices are aggregated here. Results are sorted by self-identified gender.
Source: OECD Secretariat estimates based on the OECD Risks That Matter 2020 survey, https://www.oecd.org/social/risks-that-matter.htm.

first quarter employment rate of 68.6%, before the pandemic hit most countries (OECD, 2021[8]).

This sense of insecurity at the household level also reflects the widely held understanding that national economies had deteriorated from 2019 to 2020 (Figure 1.3). A majority of respondents in every country except Lithuania report that their country's economic situation had worsened during the pandemic (in Lithuania, 47.9% say it has worsened[2]). The rate is over 80% in Spain, Portugal, Israel, Austria, Ireland and Chile.

When disaggregating risk perceptions across issue areas, RTM respondents are understandably – against the backdrop of the pandemic – very worried about their health (Figure 1.4). 61.2% of respondents, on average across countries, say they are concerned or very concerned about becoming ill or disabled in the next year or two. This is about 7 percentage points higher than the share who listed health as a top-three concern in the 2018 survey, though it should be noted that question wording changed slightly for this and some other questions (see Box 1.2 for a note on comparisons over time). In Chile, Greece, Italy, Mexico, Portugal and Spain, more than 70% of respondents list health as an issue that worries them.

Aside from health, financial worries are at the fore. On average across the sample, 54.7% of respondents are somewhat or very concerned about losing a job or self-employment income, and 58.7% are worried about being able to pay all of their expenses and making ends meet.

Long-term care (LTC) for elderly family members is a prominent concern. 56.5% of respondents, across countries, report that they are concerned or very concerned about securing good-quality long-term care for elderly family members. This concern is more widely shared across countries. In no country do fewer than 40% of respondents worry about securing long-term care for elderly family, and it is the most often-cited concern in Austria and the Netherlands (with 50.1% and 44% citing it, respectively).

The causal mechanism driving this is not clear, but it seems possible that rising concerns about long-term care reflect worries about elderly family members' well-being during the pandemic. Before the vaccine roll-out, about half of all COVID deaths in OECD countries occurred among residents of LTC institutions (OECD, 2021[9]). Concerns about finding good-quality LTC may also reflect demographic trends and population ageing in places like Greece, Spain and Portugal – countries where over 75% of respondents express concern about long-term care for older family members, and countries which also have relatively large elderly populations vis-à-vis the total population (OECD, 2020[10]). People are also very concerned about caring for elderly relatives in countries like Chile and Mexico, which historically have had relatively low levels of formal LTC support.

Another measure of insecurity comes from the question, "If you (or your partner) lost your (their) job, for roughly how long could you and your family get by before being in serious financial trouble?" 31% of respondents,[3] on average across countries, report that they would not last three months before being in serious financial trouble, with rates over 40% in Chile, Greece, Mexico (with the highest share: 56.8%), Poland, Turkey and the United States. When looking only at households that have not experienced any outright job loss during COVID-19, the

Figure 1.3. Seven out of ten people in OECD countries see a deterioration of their country's economic situation since 2019

Percent of respondents who say that their country's economic situation is worse or much worse than it was 12 months ago, 2020

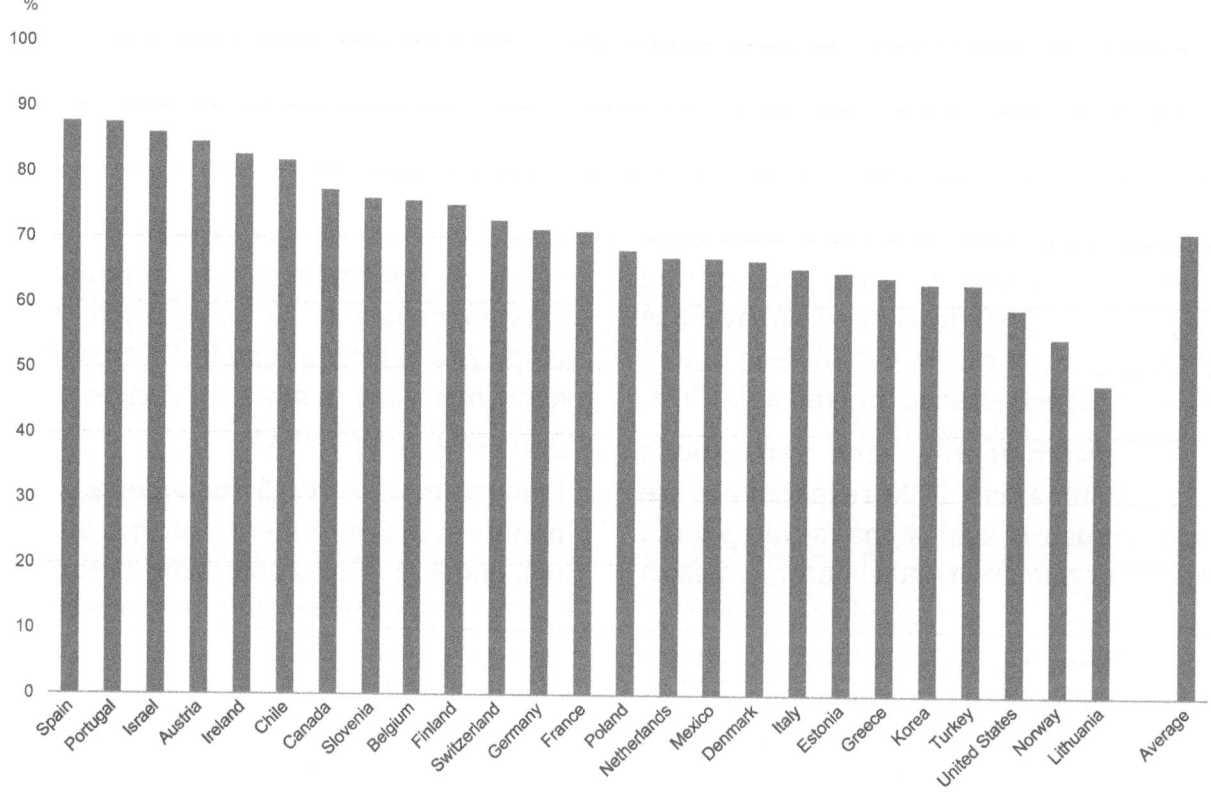

Note: Respondents were asked "Do you think that your country's economic situation is better than, the same as, or worse than it was 12 months ago?" Answer choices were "much worse," "worse," "about the same," "better," "much better" and "cannot choose." The percentages here are an aggregation of the responses "worse" and "much worse."
Source: OECD Secretariat estimates based on the OECD Risks That Matter 2020 survey, https://www.oecd.org/social/risks-that-matter.htm

cross-national average drops only slightly, to 29.7%.

Economic insecurity is again a prominent concern for women, while health concerns are for men. In ten countries, making ends meet is the risk that the highest share of women state that they are concerned or very concerned about. The risk of illness or disability comes out as the most commonly cited concern among men in 11 countries.

Figure 1.4. People are most concerned about their health and making ends meet
Percent of respondents indicating they are somewhat concerned or very concerned by each identified risk, 2020

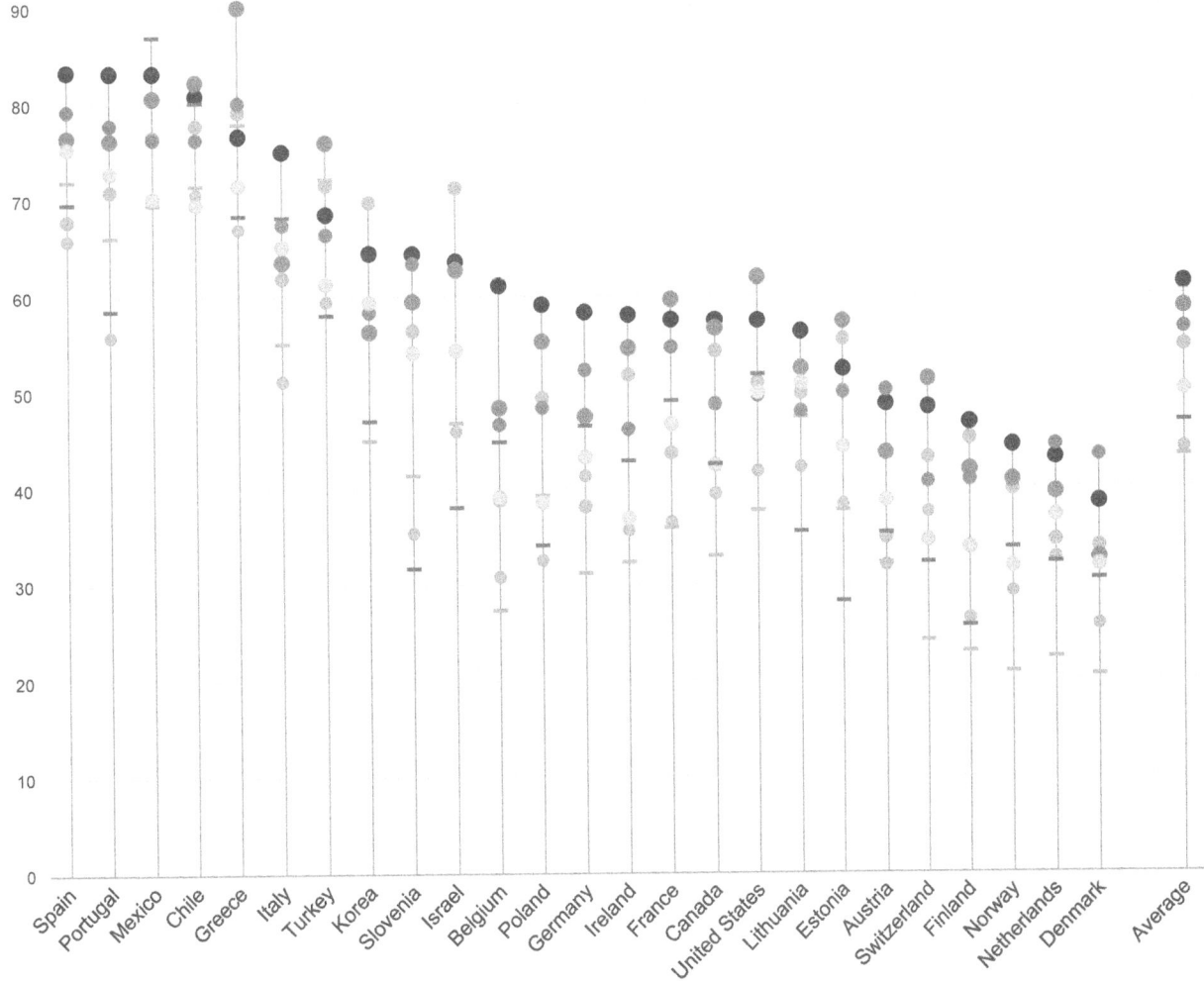

Note: Respondents were asked to rate the risks to themselves or their immediate family from a list of nine risks. Respondents had the option of selecting not at all concerned, not so concerned, somewhat concerned, very concerned or can't choose. Percentages shown here present the aggregation of "somewhat concerned" and "very concerned" answer choices.
Source: OECD Secretariat estimates based on the OECD Risks That Matter 2020 survey, https://www.oecd.org/social/risks-that-matter.htm.

Box 1.1. About the OECD Risks that Matter Survey

The OECD Risks that Matter (RTM) survey is a cross-national survey examining people's perceptions of the social and economic risks they face and how well they think their government addresses those risks. The survey was conducted for the first time in two waves in the spring and autumn of 2018. The 2020 survey, conducted in September-October 2020, draws on a representative sample of over 25 000 people aged 18 to 64 years old in 25 OECD countries: Austria, Belgium, Canada, Chile, Denmark, Estonia, Finland, France, Germany, Greece, Ireland, Israel, Italy, Korea, Lithuania, Mexico, the Netherlands, Norway, Poland, Portugal, Slovenia, Spain, Switzerland, Turkey and the United States. Respondents were asked about their social and economic concerns, how well they think government responds to their needs and expectations, and what policies they would like to see in the future.

The aim of the survey is to understand better what citizens want and need from social policy. Standard data sources, such as administrative records and labour force surveys, provide traditional data on issues such as where and how much people work, how much they earn, their health status, whether or not they are in education, and even, in the case of time-use surveys, how much they sleep and how they choose to spend their free time. These traditional surveys have been invaluable for social policy research and have helped shape social programmes for decades.

Yet these traditional data sources rarely illuminate people's concerns, perceived vulnerabilities and preferences, especially with regard to government policy. Existing cross-national surveys in this area (such as certain rounds of the International Social Survey Programme or the European Commission's Eurobarometer survey) are conducted infrequently and/or only in specific regions. The OECD Risks that Matter survey fills this gap – it complements existing data sources by providing comparable OECD-wide information on people's opinions about risks and social policies.

The survey questionnaire was developed in consultation with OECD member countries. RTM principally covers 1) risk perceptions and the economic challenges facing respondents and their households; 2) satisfaction with social protection and government; and 3) preferences for social protection going forward. The 2020 survey questionnaire has added subsections on experiences during COVID-19, the future of work, and inequality. Most questions are fixed-response, taking the form of either binary-response or scale-response. The questionnaire is conducted in national languages.

Consistent with similar surveys, RTM is implemented online using non-probability samples recruited via the internet and over the phone. The survey contractor is Respondi Ltd. Respondents are paid a nominal sum of around one or two euros per survey. Sampling is conducted through quotas, with sex, age group, education level, income level, and employment status (in the last quarter of 2019) used as the sampling criteria. Survey weights are used to correct for any under- or over-representation based on these five criteria. The target and weighted sample is 1 000 respondents per country. While COVID-19 infection was not used as a quota target, Secretariat analyses show a strong and statistically significant relationship cross-nationally between self-reported COVID-19 infection rates in RTM and epidemiological data from October 2020.

RTM is overseen by the OECD Employment, Labour and Social Affairs Committee (ELSAC). This oversight includes a regular review process by Delegates and included a technical workshop for Delegates in December 2019. Financial support for the survey was provided by OECD member countries' voluntary contributions, the OECD Secretariat, and researchers at the University of Lausanne and the University of Konstanz.

Figure 1.5. Financial security is women's most-often cited concern in many countries, while health is for men

Percent of respondents indicating they are somewhat concerned or very concerned by each identified risk, sorted by the most-often cited risk in each country and by gender, 2020

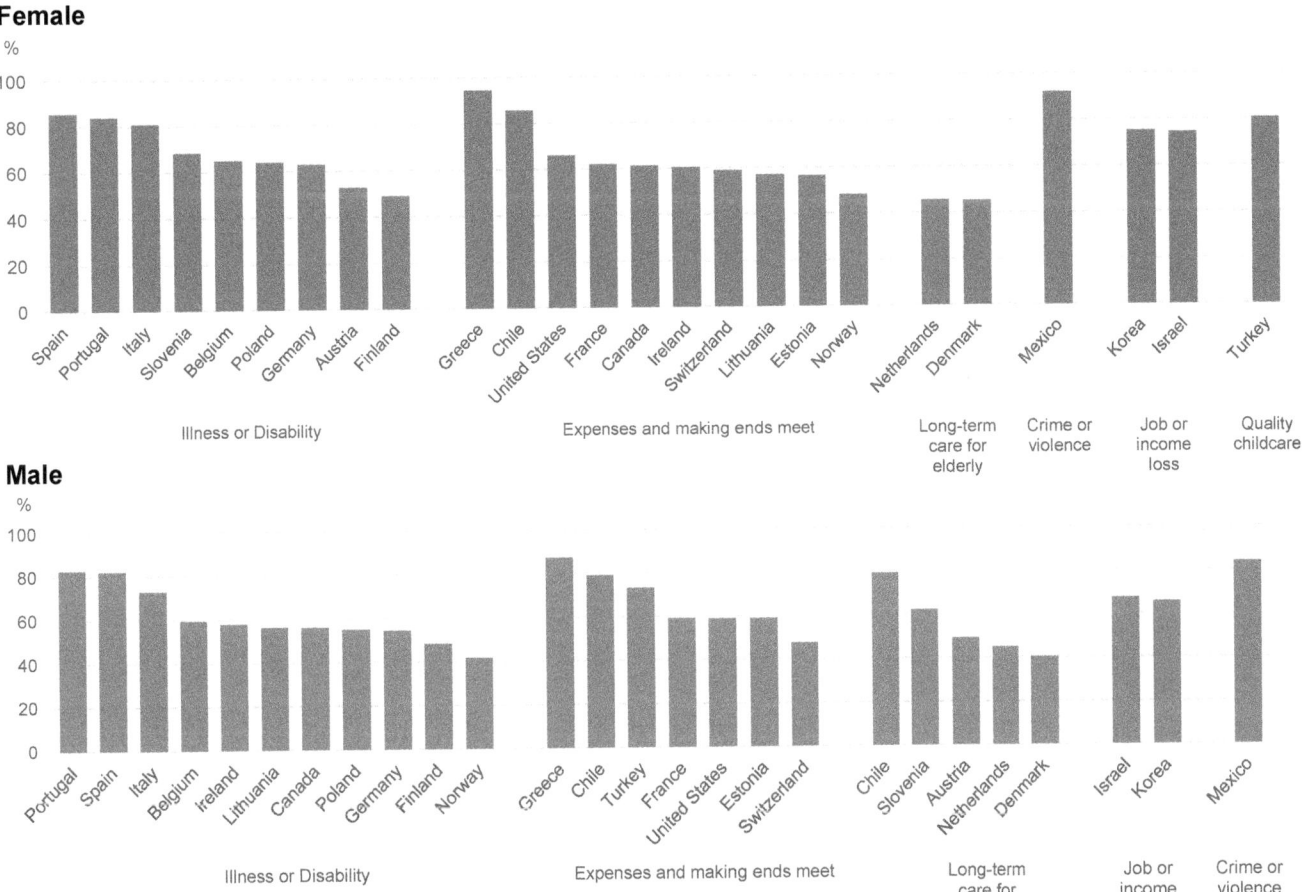

Note: Respondents were asked to rate the risks to themselves or their immediate family from a list of nine risks (listed in Figure 1.4). Respondents had the option of selecting not at all concerned, not so concerned, somewhat concerned, very concerned or can't choose. Percentages shown here present the aggregation of "somewhat concerned" and "very concerned" answer choices, sorted by the most-cited concern in each country and by gender.
Source: OECD Secretariat estimates based on the OECD Risks That Matter 2020 survey, https://www.oecd.org/social/risks-that-matter.htm

Given widespread school and childcare closures around the world, it is unsurprising that parents are highly worried about accessing good-quality childcare or education for their children. On average, 63.1% of parents (with children under age 12) are concerned or very concerned about accessing good-quality childcare or education, with rates over 70% in Chile, Greece, Spain, Mexico, Turkey, Portugal and Italy. This may reflect deeper issues around responsibilities for unpaid care work during the pandemic, when many formal institutions closed (OECD, forthcoming). Among people without children, and parents of older children, not surprisingly, only 37.2% are worried about accessing good-quality childcare or education for children or young family members.

Different degrees of worry about economic insecurity also arise when disaggregating the sample by income. Lower-income respondents, defined as those in the lowest three (national) income deciles (Figure 1.6.), are much more worried about job insecurity and making ends meet than the rest of the sample. On average across countries, 70.1% of respondents in the bottom three national income deciles are worried about expenses and making ends meet, compared to 57.5% of the middle-income earners and 47.6% in the top three deciles. Making ends meet is the top concern for low-income respondents in 17 countries.

Figure 1.6. Low-income respondents are very worried about making ends meet

Percent of respondents indicating they are somewhat concerned or very concerned by each identified risk, sorted by the most-often cited risk in each country and by income grouping, 2020

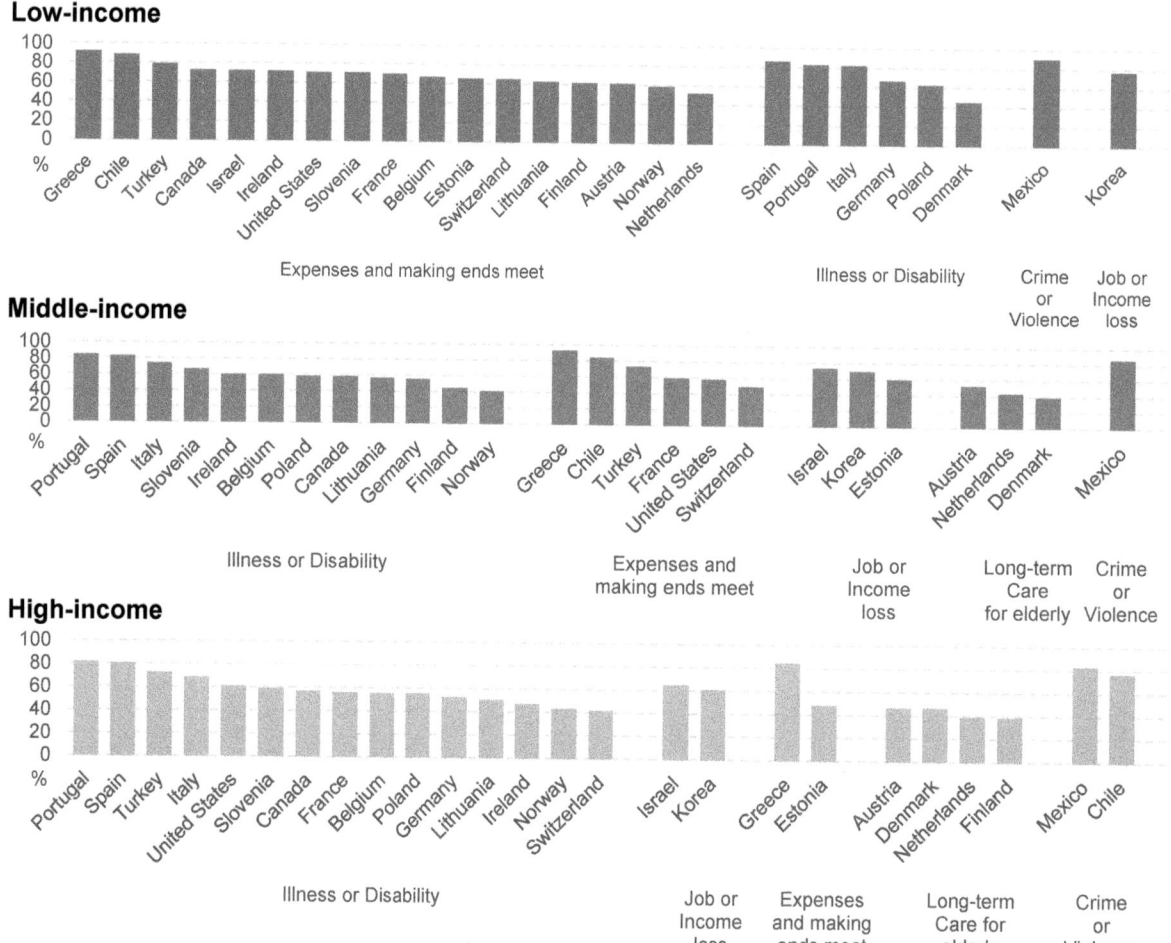

Note: Respondents were asked to rate the risks to themselves or their immediate family from a list of nine risks (listed in Figure 1.4). Respondents had the option of selecting not at all concerned, not so concerned, somewhat concerned, very concerned or can't choose. Percentages shown here present the aggregation of "somewhat concerned" and "very concerned" answer choices, sorted by the most-cited concern in each country and by income grouping. Respondents from "low income" households are defined as those in households with disposable (equivalised) incomes in the bottom three deciles of the national disposable income distribution (latest year available), respondents from "middle income" households are defined as those in households with disposable (equivalised) incomes in the middle four deciles of the national disposable income distribution (latest year available), and respondents from "high income" households those with disposable (equivalised) incomes in the top three deciles of the national disposable income distribution.
Source: OECD Secretariat estimates based on the OECD Risks That Matter 2020 survey, https://www.oecd.org/social/risks-that-matter.htm

1.2. Retirement, health and long-term care dominate long-term perspectives

In the long run – beyond the next decade – risk perceptions are focused on health and financial outcomes. 73.1% of respondents say that they are somewhat or very concerned about not being in good health, on average across countries (Figure 1.7). This prioritisation is not dramatically different from results in RTM 2018, perhaps because worries about health problems in the long run should be a fairly constant concern over time.

Pensions remain a major concern, as well. 71.9% of respondents are somewhat or very concerned about financial security in old age, with rates over 80% in Chile (89.6%), Greece (88.3%), Mexico (86.6%), Portugal (88.3%) and Spain (87.9%). Worries about financial security in old age are lowest in northern Europe, with rates below 60% in Denmark (48.3%), Finland (57%), the Netherlands (53.8%) and Norway (55.3%) – although it is worth nothing that these are still sizeable shares of the population.

Long-term care is again a major source of concern when respondents look beyond the next decade. 64.5% of respondents say they worry about not being able to access good-quality long-term care for themselves, and 64.4% worry about accessing good-quality long-term care for an elderly family member. This is also one of the issues where people are least satisfied with public programmes and income support in the event that a family member needs to stop working to provide long-term care (Chapter 3).

Figure 1.7. Falling ill, financial security in old age and long-term care are top worries in the long run

Percent of respondents indicating they are concerned or very concerned about each of the noted issue areas, 2020

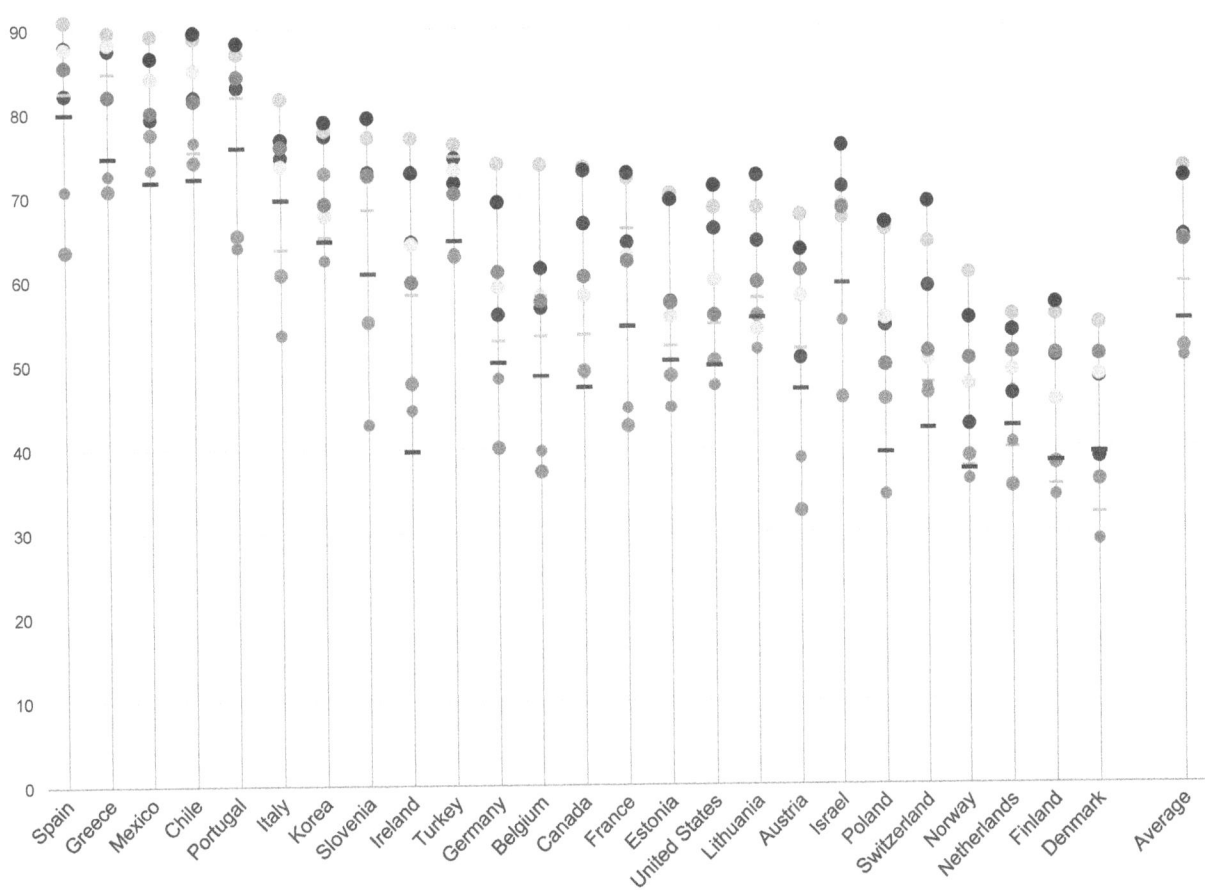

Note: Respondents were asked to rate the risks to themselves or their immediate family from a list of nine risks. Respondents had the option of selecting not at all concerned, not so concerned, somewhat concerned, very concerned or can't choose. Percentages shown here present the aggregation of "somewhat concerned" and "very concerned" answer choices.
Source: OECD Secretariat estimates based on the OECD Risks That Matter 2020 survey, https://www.oecd.org/social/risks-that-matter.htm

> "The social risk for many [during the pandemic] is loneliness. The economic risk is the disappearance of the self-employed middle class. This is where the government must continue to invest in people like self-employed workers and artists, so that they can continue to survive."
>
> – 62 year old man, Belgium

Box 1.2. A note on comparisons between RTM 2018 and RTM 2020

Changes in results between the 2018 and 2020 RTM waves should be interpreted with caution, as there are important differences in the questionnaire and sampling across the two waves. Some of the question wording changed between survey waves. In the section on risk perceptions, for instance, respondents in 2018 were asked to identify and rank the top three risks that they face from a list of choices. In 2020, respondents were asked to rate their degree of concern about every listed issue on a Likert scale. It is therefore difficult to make straightforward comparisons for these questions, but in general there are strong correlations in country ordering over time for top risks and there are few dramatic shifts for other repeat questions.

The Risks that Matter survey also uses a cross-sectional sample of respondents that do not repeat over time. The change in sample implies some observable differences between sample respondents. One difference between the samples, for example, is that the upper age bound in 2018 was 70 years old, whereas the upper age bound in 2020 is 64 years old.[4] Another major difference is the inclusion of four additional countries that were not enrolled in the 2018 study: Korea, Spain, Switzerland and Turkey.

1.3. Risk perceptions are well founded

Respondents' worries about financial security are well founded.

Households in OECD countries have experienced a high degree of economic insecurity during COVID-19.[5] On average across countries, 11.8% of respondents to RTM 2020 worldwide report that either they or a household member have lost a job or lost their own business since the start of the crisis, with rates over 20% in Chile, Mexico and Turkey (Figure 1.8).

However, outright job loss represents only a small portion of the total economic disruption experienced by households. More than one-third (37.3%) of all respondents to RTM 2020 say that either they or a household member have experienced at least one job-related disruption in the form of a job loss, a job lay-off, the use of a job-retention scheme, a working hours reduction, and/or a pay cut, on average, across countries. When (paid or unpaid) leave-takings and resignations are included, a total of 44.2% of respondents have experienced some kind of job-related disruption in their household during the pandemic (OECD, 2021$_{[1]}$).

Youths (aged 18 to 29), parents with children under age 18 in the house, and lower-income workers report experiencing more job disruptions than other groups and have high levels of financial insecurity (OECD, 2021$_{[1]}$; 2021$_{[11]}$).

Employment figures are best derived from traditional, regular labour force surveys (LFS) and administrative data like tax records. RTM cannot be directly compared with LFS results for a few reasons. One issue is that RTM asks about job loss in the household, rather than simply the respondent. RTM also asks a retrospective question that covers having experienced disruptions over a period of several months, from March to

October 2020, which does not track with any traditional LFS figures (e.g. a monthly or quarterly unemployment rate). RTM is fundamentally a survey on perceptions, and the background questions on job disruption are intended to help present a snapshot of what was happening in households during the pandemic. This picture reveals that RTM 2020 respondents are showing a high degree of financial stress – a picture that is consistent with other, more traditional data sources (OECD, 2020[2]; 2021[8]).

Figure 1.8. Almost half of all households have suffered some form of job-related disruption

Percent of respondents reporting that either they or a member of their household have/has lost a job (including self-employment/own business), and percent reporting any form of job-related disruption in the household, since the start of the COVID-19 pandemic, 2020

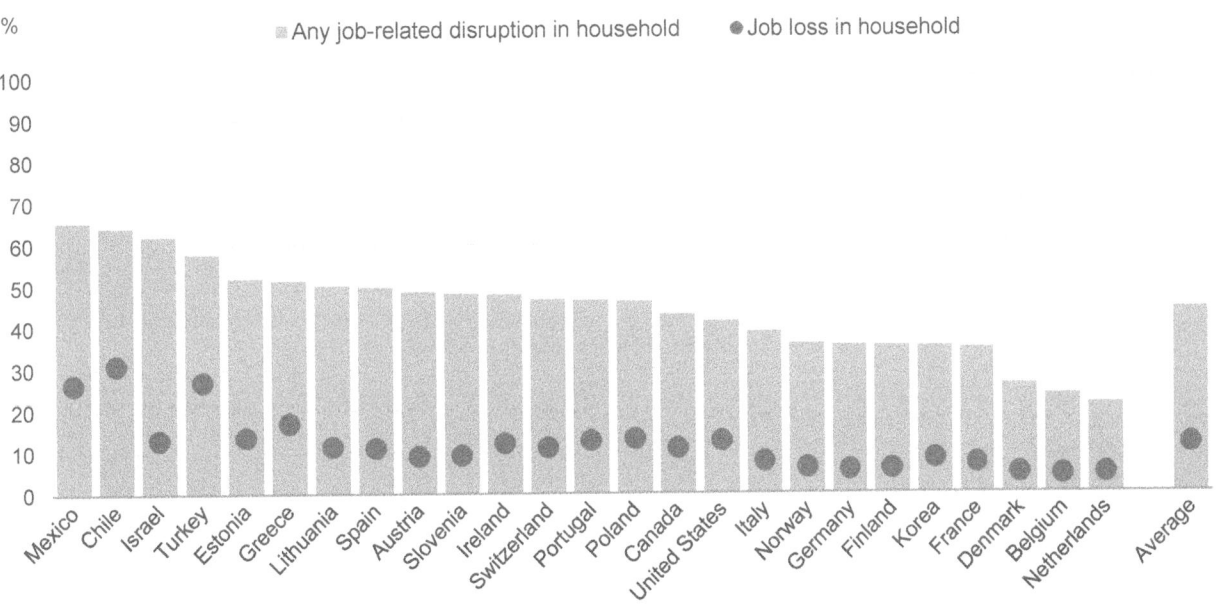

Note: Respondents were asked whether, at any time since the start of the COVID-19 pandemic, they (or any member of their household) had experienced one or more of a range of specific employment-related events. The options were: lost job, lost self-employed job, or lost own business; laid off temporarily or place on a job retention scheme; had working hours reduced or place on a part-time job retention scheme; had pay reduced by employer or lost income form self-employed job or own business; took leave from work (paid or unpaid); resigned from job. Respondents could select all the options that applied. Percentages present the share of respondents who selected at least one.
Source: OECD Secretariat estimates based on the OECD Risks That Matter 2020 survey, https://www.oecd.org/social/risks-that-matter.htm

These job losses, cuts in work hours and pay, placements on job retention schemes, and leave-takings have, in turn, made it harder for many households to pay even their usual bills.

Close to one-third of all respondents (31%) report that they or their household experienced at least one of the following financial difficulties since the start of the pandemic (Figure 1.9):

- failed to pay a usual expense;
- took money out of savings or sold assets to pay for usual expense;
- took money from family or friends to pay for a usual expense;

- took on additional debt or used credit to pay for usual expenses;
- asked a charity or non-profit organisation for assistance because they could not afford to pay;
- went hungry because they could not afford to pay for food;
- lost their home because they could not afford the mortgage or rent;
- declared bankruptcy or asked a credit provider for help.

For a disaggregation of the frequency of these financial difficulties by country, please see Annex Table 1.

Among those respondents whose household experienced job loss during COVID, the share who had financial difficulty jumps to 67.7%, on average, across countries.

These national averages correspond with rates found in other surveys carried out during COVID-19, even if questions differ slightly (see, for example, surveys of European Union countries and the United States (European Parliament / Eurobarometer, 2020[12]; Carman and Nataraj, 2020[13]).

Figure 1.9. Almost one-third of respondents report financial difficulties since the start of the crisis

Share of respondents reporting at least one financial difficulty since the start of the COVID-19 pandemic, by reported experience of job loss in the household since the start of the pandemic, 2020

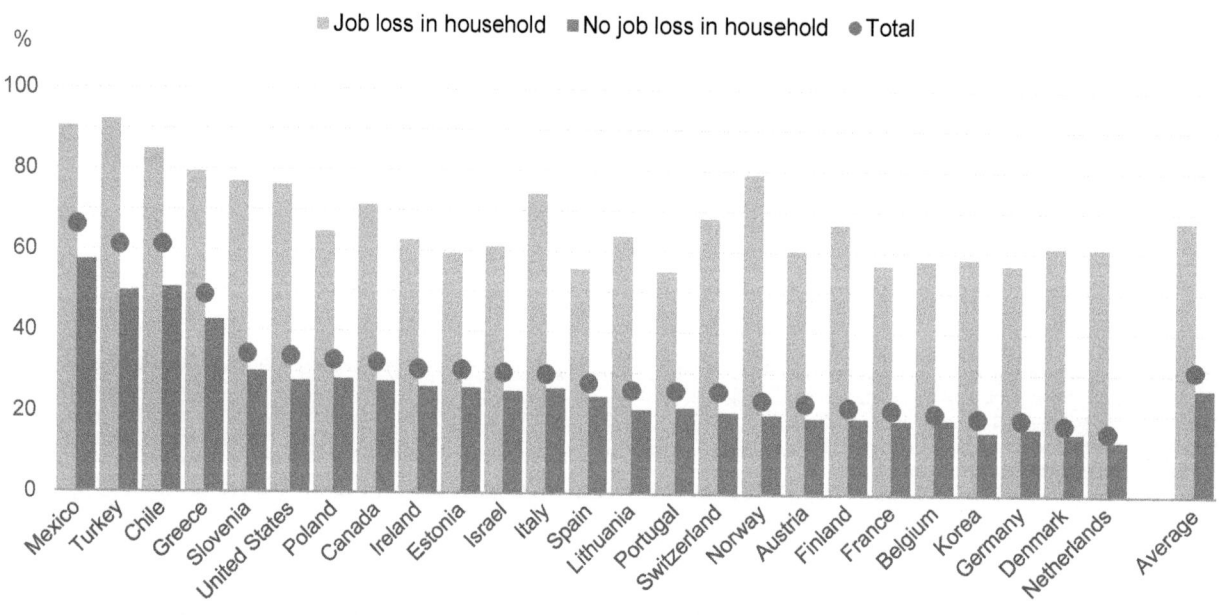

Note: Respondents were asked whether, at any time since the start of the COVID-19 pandemic, they (or their household) had experienced one or more of a range of specific finance-related events: failed to pay a usual expense, took money out of savings or sold assets to pay for a usual expense, took money from family or friends to pay for a usual expense, took on additional debt or used credit to pay for a usual expense, asked a charity or non-profit organisation for assistance because they could not afford to pay, went hungry because they could not afford to pay for food, lost their home because they could not afford the mortgage or rent, or declared bankruptcy or asked a credit provider for help. Respondents could select all the options that applied; percentages present the share of respondents who selected at least one. "Job loss in household" refers to respondents reporting that either they or any member of their household have/ has either "Lost their job or been laid off permanently by their employer" and/or "Lost their self-employed job or their own business", since the start of the COVID-19 pandemic. Note that the majority of households without outright job loss nevertheless had some other type of job disruption.
Source: OECD Secretariat estimates based on the OECD Risks That Matter 2020 survey, https://www.oecd.org/social/risks-that-matter.htm

The degree of economic hardship varies across countries. Respondents in wealthier countries and those with historically higher levels of spending on social programmes reveal less financial stress (Figure 1.10). Among the 25 surveyed countries, those that have higher levels of GDP per capita (Figure 1.10, Panel A) and those that historically spent more on social programmes (Figure 1.10, Panel B) tend also to have fewer respondents reporting financial difficulties in the household since the start of the COVID-19.

These associations are driven in part by the high reported levels of financial stress in Chile, Mexico and Turkey – all countries with lower levels of social spending and GDP per capita, compared to the OECD average. These are also the countries with the highest levels of labour market informality in the OECD, meaning that many workers are excluded from contributory social protection schemes. But even if these three countries are discounted, reported financial stress is higher where pre-crisis GDP per capita and pre-crisis public social spending were lower.

Figure 1.10. Financial difficulties less common in richer countries and those with larger social safety nets

Percent of respondents reporting experience of financial difficulties in the household since the start of the COVID-19 pandemic, GDP per capita (USD 2015 PPP), and total public social expenditure per capita (USD 2015 PPP)

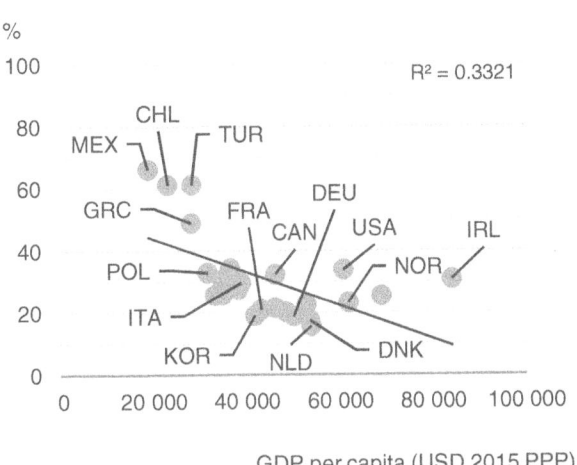
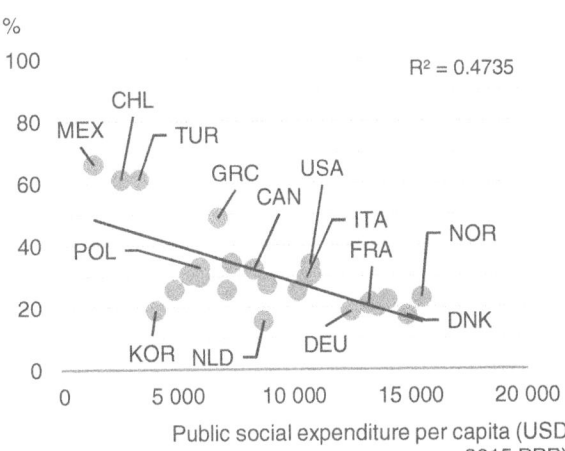

Note: Respondents were asked whether, at any time since the start of the COVID-19 pandemic, they (or their household) had experienced one or more of a range of specific finance-related events. Respondents could select all the options that applied. Data on GDP per capita refer to 2019. Data on total public social expenditure per head refer to 2017, except for Switzerland (2016).
Source: OECD Secretariat estimates based on the OECD Risks That Matter 2020 survey, https://www.oecd.org/social/risks-that-matter.htm, OECD National Accounts, http://www.oecd.org/sdd/na/, and the OECD Social Expenditure Database, https://www.oecd.org/social/expenditure.htm.

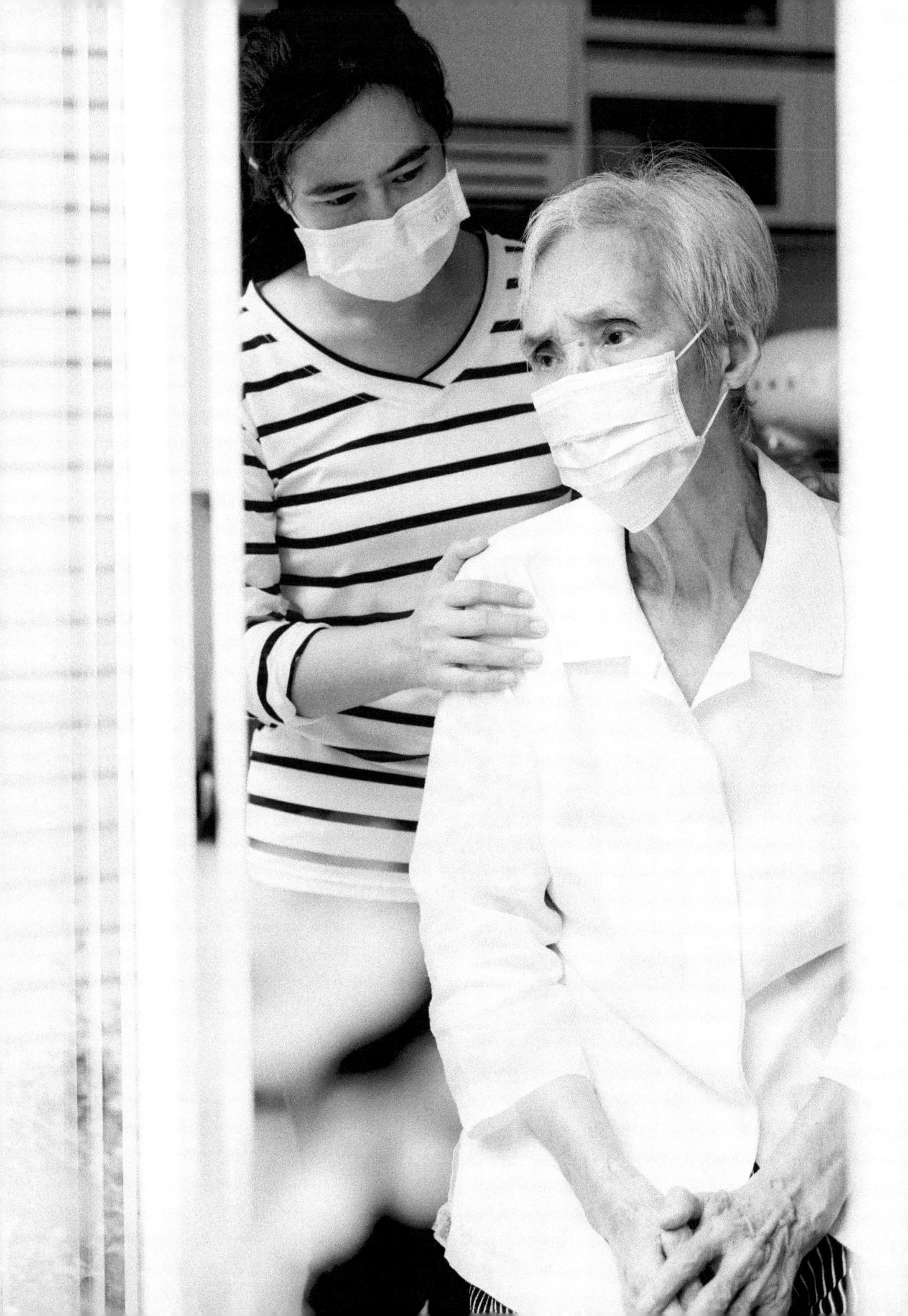

2. Is social protection working?

2.1. A social contract for a pandemic

"Even before the COVID pandemic hit we didn't have a lot of extra cash, and it has only gotten worse since the start of it."

– 60-year-old man, Canada

The growth of spending on social protection in OECD countries during 2020 will almost certainly represent the largest peacetime expansion of OECD welfare states in nearly a century. Spending data are still coming in, and it is still difficult to measure the exact sizes and shapes of social programmes that emerged during COVID-19. It is also hard to say which measures will end up being temporary and which will have staying power. But it is beyond dispute that the expansion has been enormous.

Throughout the OECD, national governments have rolled out enhanced income support, family benefits, child benefits, unemployment insurance, health care, pension supplements and housing supports to help households get through the pandemic (OECD, 2021[14], 2020[4], 2020[6], ISSA, 2021[7], Gentilini et al., 2021[15]). Many subnational governments, too, enacted their own measures. These investments came on top of many other policy measures intended to safeguard households that did not necessarily require public funding, such as eviction bans.

Considerable effort has been focused on protecting jobs and ensuring adequate household income during lockdowns or strict confinement periods, when economic activities were reduced dramatically. These measures took the form of short-time work schemes or wage subsidies aimed at reducing labour costs, preventing a surge in unemployment, and mitigating financial hardship by supporting the income of people working reduced hours (though usually below a 100% income replacement rate) (OECD, 2020[4]). By May 2020, job retention (JR) schemes were supporting about 50 million jobs across many OECD countries – about ten times as many as during the global financial crisis in 2008-09 (OECD, 2020[4]).

How were these and other measures perceived by people living in OECD countries?

2.2. Low public confidence in income support

Despite the massive public investments made during the pandemic, people's confidence in the ability of their government to support them through financial difficulties is low. Only 35.8% of respondents say they have confidence that government would sufficiently support them in the case of financial difficulties. The Netherlands has the highest share believing that they can count on government, at 56.1%. In contrast, nearly six out of ten respondents across countries – 59.3% – say that they have little or no confidence that cash benefits and services provided by their government would sufficiently support them if they were to experience financial difficulties.

Personal networks, instead, play a key role. A majority of respondents across countries – 52.5% – expect that a friend or family member would be able and willing to help out in a period of financial difficulty, with respondents in Austria, Germany, Spain and the United States expressing the highest levels of confidence in support from these kinds of personal networks. In Estonia, Israel, Portugal and Spain, there are particularly large gaps between the share of people who believe friends and family would help them, relative to government. In Spain, for example, 60.6% of respondents say that friends and family would help them through financial difficulties, while only 21.8% say that they would count on government.

Perceptions across countries are not always connected with actual levels of government intervention during the crisis. France, for example, offered a job retention scheme that paid a replacement rate of 70% (at the average wage) during the crisis, up to a ceiling of EUR 4 849 monthly, and an unemployment benefit equal to 57% of the average wage (OECD, 2021[3]). About 35% of dependent employed French workers took up the short-time work scheme in April-May 2020. Yet less than a third (30.5%) of RTM 2020 respondents in France say they are confident that the government would provide cash benefits or services sufficient to get them through the financial difficulties. In contrast, 38.5% of Belgians have confidence that the government would help them through financial troubles, even though Belgium offered a job retention scheme that paid a lower replacement rate than France (of 50% of the average wage), up to a lower ceiling (EUR 2 100 monthly), and the enrolment of dependent workers in April-May 2020 was lower than in France. Belgium also offered a lower unemployment benefit, equal to 42% of the average wage (OECD, 2021[3]).

Figure 2.1. People count on friends and family – more than government – to support them through financial difficulty

Percent of respondents indicating they are somewhat confident or very confident in different sources providing support in case of financial trouble, 2020

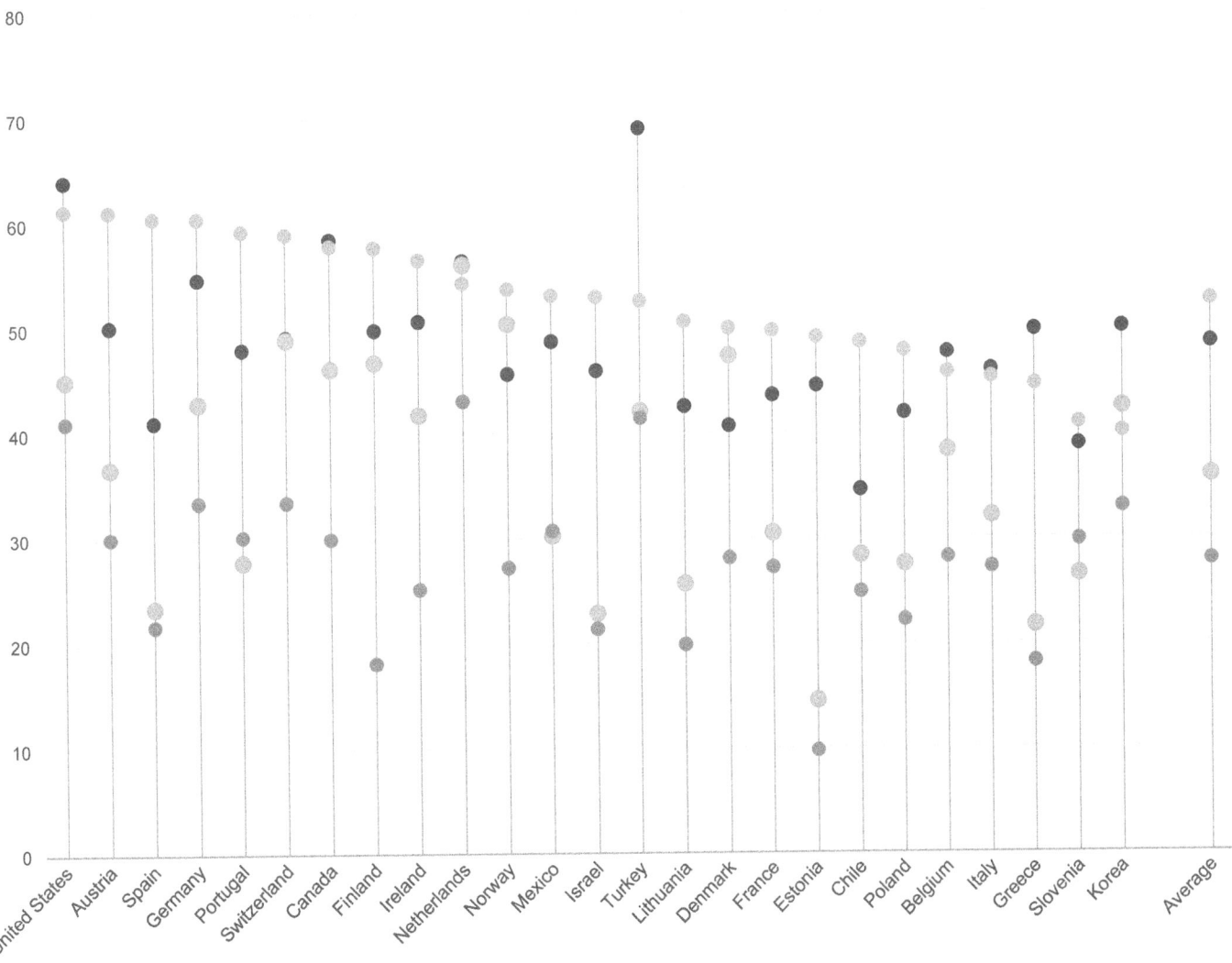

Note: Respondents were asked how confident they were that they could turn to various forms of support should they experience financial trouble. The response options were "not at all confident", "not so confident", "somewhat confident", "very confident" for each answer choice. Respondents could also choose "can't choose" as a response option. Response options "somewhat confident" and "very confident" are aggregated here.
Source: OECD Secretariat estimates based on the OECD Risks That Matter 2020 survey, https://www.oecd.org/social/risks-that-matter.htm

When looking at specific life events, respondents are generally quite sceptical that the government would (or does) provide them or their household with adequate income support during periods with major income losses. People are most likely to agree that government would provide them with adequate income support in the case of unemployment, though these rates are still low. Across countries, 27.5% of respondents say that they think government would (or does) provide adequate income supports in the event of unemployment, with rates as high as 40.9% in Switzerland and as low as 11.9% in Chile.

Financial security in old age is another area in which people think government falls short. Only 22.6% of respondents, cross-nationally, feel that government would or does provide adequate income replacement during retirement, while 48.8% of respondents say that government would not provide adequate income replacement. While there is a slight positive correlation between the degree of relative old-age income poverty and people's scepticism about the adequacy of government income support (Figure 2.2), there is almost no cross-national relationship between projected replacement rates for pensions and perceptions of government adequacy in old-age income support. Indeed, countries with similar degrees of scepticism often have very different levels of pension generosity. In Portugal, for example, 61.5% of respondents say they do not feel that government provides adequate income security in old age, even as the future pension replacement rate is 89.6%[6]. Respondents are similarly sceptical about government income supports in old age in Lithuania (59.8%), despite the pension replacement rate being much lower (31%).

Public confidence is lowest when considering income support for long-term care. Across countries, only 17.9% of respondents say that they agree or strongly agree that the government would (or does) provide adequate income support if they had to leave work to care for elderly family members or family members with disabilities. In Chile, Estonia, Finland, Greece, Israel, Lithuania, Mexico and Portugal, fewer than 15% of respondents say that they think government would (or does) provide them with adequate income support in the event of leaving work to care for elderly family members or family members with disability. In contrast, 51% of people across countries report the opposite: they disagree or strongly disagree that government would or does provide adequate income support for leaving-work to care for elderly family members or family members with disability.

Figure 2.2. Little cross-national relationship between confidence in old-age income supports and pension replacement rates

Relative income poverty rate for 66- to 75-year-olds (%), net mandatory and voluntary projected pension replacement rate (% of pre-retirement earnings), and percentage that disagree (or strongly disagree) that the government would provide adequate income support in the case of income loss due to old-age

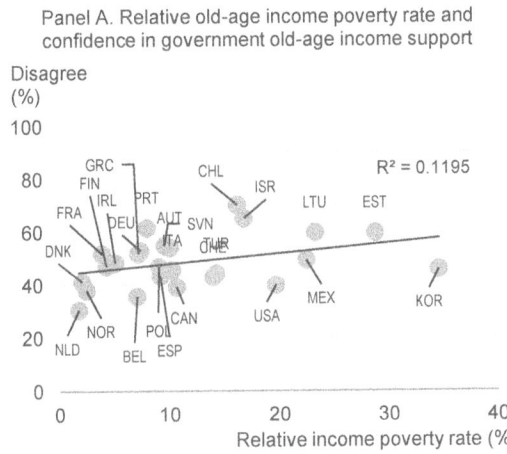
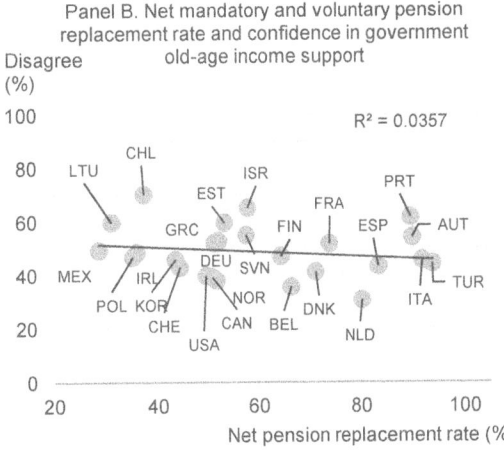

Note: Respondents were asked about the degree to which they agree or disagree with the statement "I think that the government would (or does) provide my family and me with adequate income support in the case of income loss due to old-age". Response options were "agree", "strongly agree", "disagree", "strongly disagree" and "undecided". Data on the relative income poverty rate for 66- to 75-year-olds are based on equivalised household disposable income, i.e. income after taxes and transfers adjusted for household size. The poverty threshold is set at 50% of median disposable income in each country. Data refer to 2018 or 2017, except for Mexico and the Netherlands (2016). Data on the future net pension replacement rate are based on entitlements for a man on average earnings, and refer to voluntary and mandatory pensions. Data refer to 2018.
Source: OECD Secretariat estimates based on the OECD Risks That Matter survey (2018), the OECD Income Distribution Database (http://www.oecd.org/social/income-distribution-database.htm), and OECD Pensions at a Glance database.

Figure 2.3. Policy areas with the highest level of satisfaction

Percent of respondents reporting they are satisfied or very satisfied with access to the accompanying policy area, sorted by the policy area with the highest level of satisfaction in each country, 2020

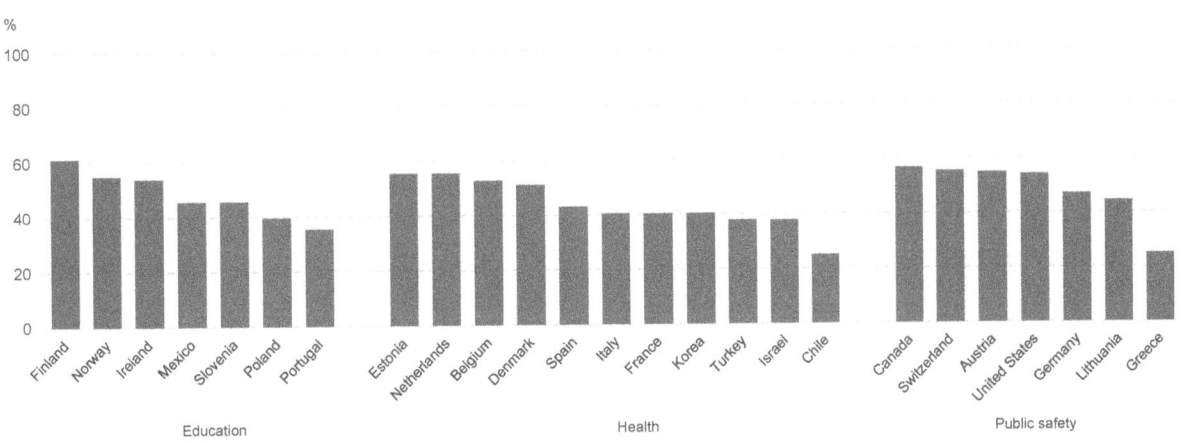

Note: Respondents were asked the degree to which they agree or disagree with the statement "I think that my family and I have access to good-quality and affordable public services in the area of…" for different areas of social policies. Possible response options were "strongly disagree," "disagree," "neither disagree nor disagree," "agree," and "strongly agree." Respondents could also choose "can't choose" as a response option. Response options "agree" and "strongly agree" are aggregated here.
Source: OECD Secretariat estimates based on the OECD Risks That Matter 2020 survey, https://www.oecd.org/social/risks-that-matter.htm.

2.3. Mixed perceptions of public programme effectiveness

Perceptions of government effectiveness vary across policy areas. RTM 2020 respondents were asked to agree or disagree with the statement, "I think that my family and I have access to good-quality and affordable public services in…" and were provided with a list of policy areas: family supports, education, employment support services, housing, health, incapacity-related needs/disability, long-term care for the elderly, and public safety.

In none of these listed issue areas do a majority of respondents, cross-nationally, feel that they have access to good-quality and affordable public services, but governments are perceived as more effective in some policy areas than others (Figure 2.3). On average across countries, people are most satisfied with public services around education, health care, and public safety in their country. 44% of respondents across countries agree or strongly agree that they have access to good-quality and affordable education (defined as schools, universities and adult learning). In Finland, over 60% of respondents are satisfied with access to good-quality and affordable education.

The second most popular programme area is health care. 43.1% of respondents cross-nationally feel that they have access to good-quality and affordable provision of health care (defined as "public medical care, subsidised health insurance, mental health support, etc."). A slim majority of respondents in Austria, Belgium, Canada, Denmark, Estonia, Finland, the Netherlands, Switzerland and the United States agree or strongly agree with having good access to health care – a noteworthy outcome considering the health exigencies of the pandemic and the stressors facing health care providers in this period.

41.9% of respondents cross-nationally report being satisfied with the provision of public safety (defined in RTM as policing). This is the policy area with the highest level of satisfaction in Austria, Canada, Germany, Greece, Lithuania, Switzerland and the United States (Figure 2.3).

People are least satisfied with public services supporting housing. Only 27.1% of respondents cross-nationally say they can access good-quality and affordable housing services (e.g. .social housing), and 35.6% cross-nationally report that they cannot access it. Indeed, good-quality and affordable housing services is the issue with the lowest level of public satisfaction in all but four countries. Turkey (where 39.5% of respondents say they do not have good access employment services like job search supports and skills training), Chile (where 51.5% say they do not have access to good-quality and affordable family supports like childcare), Denmark (where 24.7% say they do not have access to good-quality and affordable long-term care for elderly people) and Mexico (where 39.8% say they do not have access to good-quality public safety, e.g. policing) are the only countries where people are more dissatisfied with a public service other than housing support.

Housing policy is an area that has received a good deal of public attention during COVID-19, reflecting concerns around housing affordability and evictions, and governments have introduced a raft of measures to try to help people stay in their homes through the economic and health crisis. Yet most of these measures have been temporary fixes that do little to address the structural challenges driving overall housing unaffordability, such as insufficient supply (OECD, 2021[14]).

2.4. Whose programme is this? Public opinion about programme design

Citizens' feeling that they are excluded from policy design and reform is not a new issue (OECD, 2019[16]), and the pandemic has done little to change this. Respondents were asked to indicate the degree to which they agreed or disagreed with the statement "I feel the government incorporates the views of people like me when designing or reforming public benefits."

On average across countries, 49.2% of RTM 2020 respondents say that they disagree or strongly disagree that the government incorporates their views or the views of people like them. This is a slightly more positive impression than in RTM 2018, when closer to six out of ten respondents said they disagree that government incorporates their views. The addition of Korea and Switzerland to the 2020 survey sample (both of which have relatively positive impressions of governments' incorporation of people's views) helps marginally to lower the cross-national average, but otherwise most of the movement from 2018 to 2020 is from the "disagree" or "strongly disagree" answer choice to the middle "neither agree nor disagree" answer choice. There is little change in the share who say that they agree or strongly agree that government does incorporate their views: only 19.4% of RTM 2020 respondents report that government incorporates their views and the views of people like them.

People also tend to be dissatisfied with the distribution of public benefits. RTM 2020 asks a series of questions about the fairness of benefit receipt: whether the respondent feels she or he gets their "fair share," whether others are getting more than they "deserve", and how easily people can access benefits.

Cross-nationally, an average of 42.4% of people say that they do not get the fair share of benefits they deserve, given the taxes and social contributions they pay. Only 24.9% say that they do get their fair share. This is an improvement since 2018, and could be driven by the policy circumstances (e.g. the expansion of government programmes during the pandemic to a broader population). As in 2018, the countries where respondents are least likely to perceive unfairness are Belgium, Norway, the Netherlands, Denmark, Canada and the United States (though these countries have changed rank order). People are most sceptical that they get their fair share of benefits in Chile (64.5%), Spain (61%) and Israel (60.3%).

There is also a widespread sense that other people get benefits without deserving them. 61.3% of respondents express this sentiment. This is largely unchanged from 2018. 84.1% of respondents in Portugal, 73.3% in Greece and around 70% in Mexico, Italy and France feel that many people get benefits they do not deserve. Respondents in Denmark, Israel, Estonia and Korea, in contrast, have relatively more charitable views of the deservingness of benefit recipients.

The question of how easily people can access benefits is especially important in an environment of heightened economic insecurity. Across countries, nearly half of the sample – 47.7% – say that they do not think they could receive public benefits if they needed them. In contrast, in five countries – the Netherlands, Norway, Canada, Denmark and the United States – more than a third of respondents report that they do think they could access benefits if they needed them. This is still a low share expressing confidence in benefit access, and it is on par with the share in those same

2. Is social protection working

Figure 2.4. Only one in five respondents feel that government incorporates their views

Percent of respondents reporting that they agree or disagree that their government incorporates the views of people like them when designing or reforming public benefits, 2020

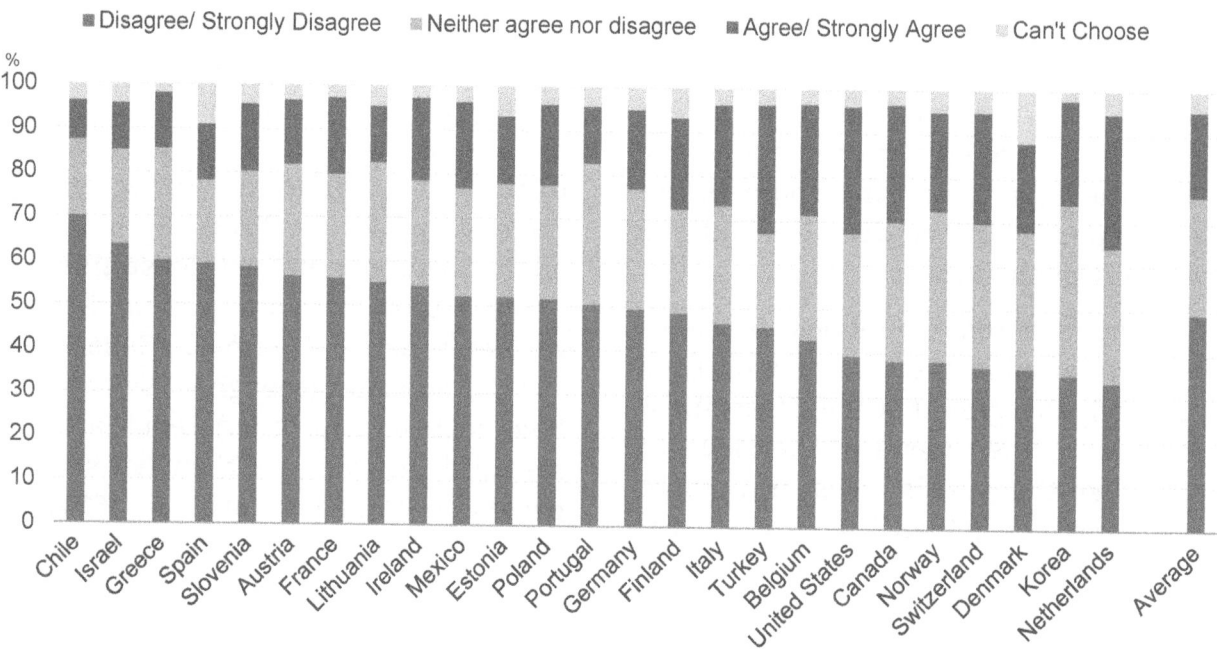

Note: Respondents were asked to what degree they feel government incorporates their views or the views of people like them. Answer choices were "strongly disagree," "disagree," "neither agree nor disagree," "agree," "strongly agree," and "cannot choose." Figure presents aggregations of "strongly disagree" with "disagree" and "agree" with "strongly agree."
Source: OECD Secretariat estimates based on the OECD Risks That Matter 2020 survey, https://www.oecd.org/social/risks-that-matter.htm

Figure 2.5. About a quarter of respondents say they get their fair share of benefits, given the taxes and social contributions they pay

Percent of respondents indicating their level of agreement with the statement "I feel I receive a fair share of public benefits, given the taxes and social contributions I pay," 2020

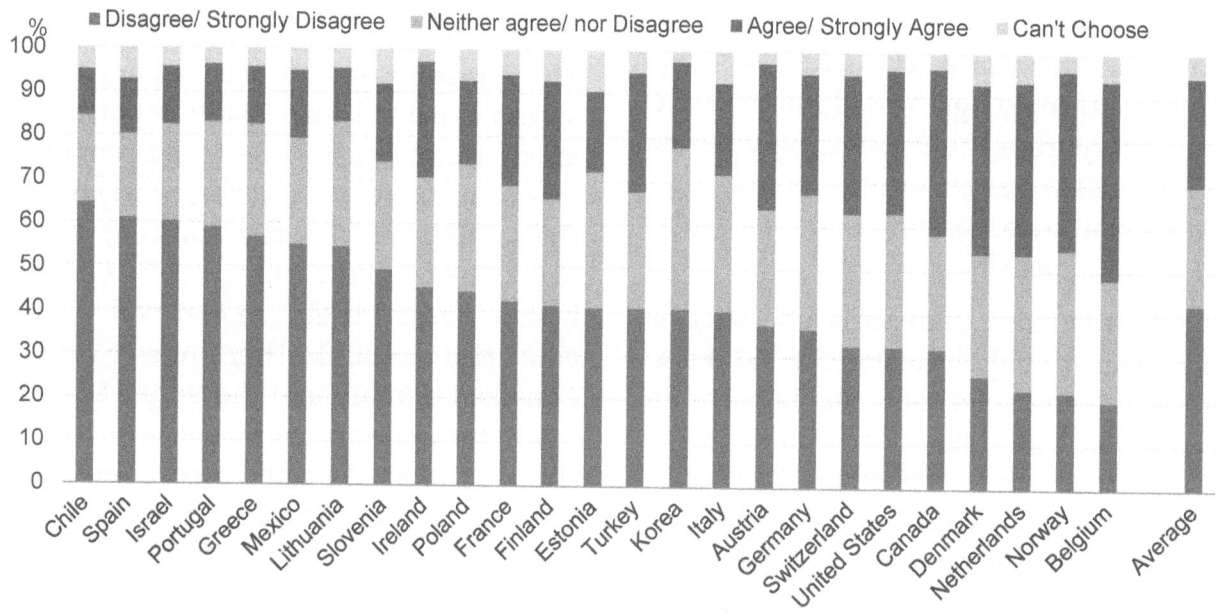

Note: Respondents were asked to indicate the degree to which they agreed or disagreed with the statement "I feel that I receive a fair share of public benefits, given the taxes and social contributions I pay". Possible response options were "strongly disagree", "disagree", "neither agree nor disagree", "agree" and "strongly agree". Respondents could also choose "can't choose".
Source: OECD Secretariat estimates based on the OECD Risks That Matter 2020 survey, https://www.oecd.org/social/risks-that-matter.htm

countries who feel they cannot access benefits.

These results raise important questions: Why do some people feel that they cannot access benefits? Does it perhaps relate to the application and enrolment process? Respondents who said they do not feel that they could easily access benefits if they needed them were asked to clarify what they perceive to be the challenge.

The most commonly cited barrier to accessing benefits, across countries, was the respondents' uncertainty about whether or not they would qualify for public benefits (Table 2.1). 57.6% of respondents cross-nationally listed this as a perceived barrier to benefit receipt, with rates as high as 74% in Korea, 73.7% in Canada, and 71.4% in Finland. The second most common barrier, cited by 54.8% of respondents cross-nationally, is the concern that the application process would be difficult, lengthy or time-consuming.

Figure 2.6. Most people think others get benefits without deserving them

Percent of respondents indicating their level of agreement with the statement "Many people receive public benefits without deserving them," 2020

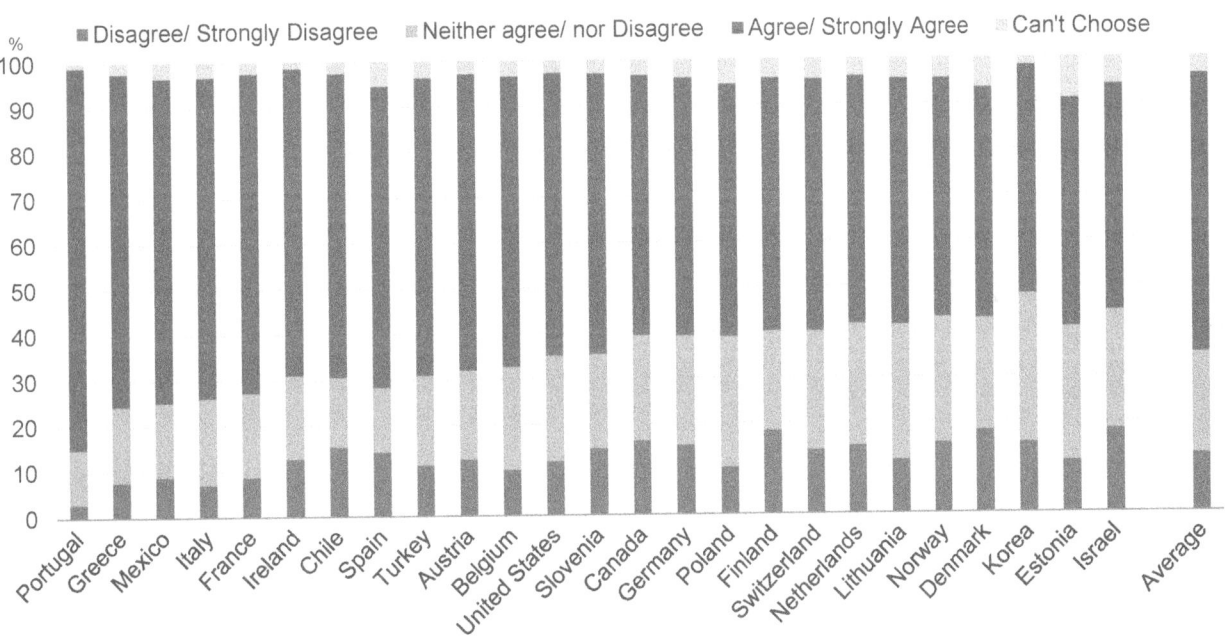

Note: Respondents were asked to indicate the degree to which they agreed or disagreed with the statement "Many people receive public benefits without deserving them". Possible response options were "strongly disagree", "disagree", "neither agree nor disagree", "agree" and "strongly agree". Respondents could also choose "can't choose".
Source: OECD Secretariat estimates based on the OECD Risks That Matter 2020 survey, https://www.oecd.org/social/risks-that-matter.htm

Figure 2.7. Most respondents feel they would not be able to receive public benefits if they needed them

Percent of respondents indicating their level of agreement with the statement "I think I could easily receive public benefits if I needed them," 2020

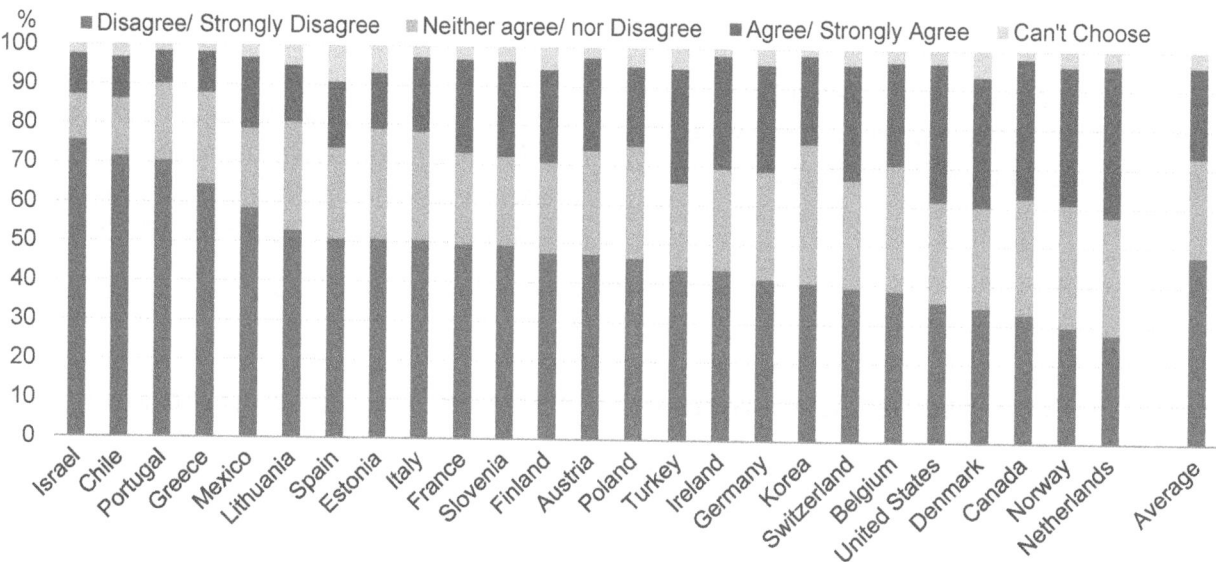

Note: Respondents were asked to indicate the degree to which they agreed or disagreed with the statement "I think I could easily receive public benefits if I needed them". Possible response options were "strongly disagree", "disagree", "neither agree nor disagree", "agree" and "strongly agree". Respondents could also choose "can't choose".
Source: OECD Secretariat estimates based on OECD Risks that Matter survey (2020).

Table 2.1. Respondents are very uncertain about their eligibility for public benefits

Percent of respondents indicating various perceived difficulties in accessing benefits, among respondents who disagreed or strongly disagreed with the statement "I believe I could access public benefits if I needed them," 2020

Country	You are not sure whether you would qualify for public benefits	You are not sure how to apply for public benefits	You think the application process would be difficult, lengthy and/or time-consuming	You are not sure that you would be treated fairly by the government office processing your claim	Other
	%	%	%	%	%
Austria	50.4	25.6	49.6	45.1	16.1
Belgium	65.0	31.8	55.7	37.5	8.4
Canada	73.7	29.0	51.5	43.1	8.5
Chile	57.8	13.6	53.8	45.3	15.3
Denmark	57.7	17.6	49.7	44.5	9.3
Estonia	62.6	33.3	56.9	52.1	4.9
Finland	71.4	14.7	41.5	25.8	12.0
France	64.8	11.0	39.0	28.4	10.6
Germany	50.8	23.0	56.0	36.9	11.8
Greece	59.8	16.8	44.8	58.8	7.5
Ireland	66.3	25.4	52.2	44.0	7.5
Israel	46.8	25.0	85.6	57.9	4.0
Italy	51.1	12.5	51.0	39.9	7.1
Korea	74.0	23.8	65.1	43.1	4.5
Lithuania	64.2	26.9	54.6	61.2	4.8
Mexico	50.8	26.5	67.9	55.4	7.2
Netherlands	62.4	13.8	52.2	33.8	8.7
Norway	41.2	19.4	73.9	49.6	6.1
Poland	61.7	25.7	58.7	57.6	3.9
Portugal	46.0	19.4	69.6	55.3	6.7
Slovenia	64.9	17.2	43.1	60.3	7.3
Spain	52.5	12.7	44.4	49.6	9.6
Switzerland	55.0	22.9	56.2	42.4	10.3
Turkey	21.3	12.6	50.2	77.0	6.5
United States	69.0	30.3	46.8	40.1	9.3
Average	57.6	21.2	54.8	47.4	8.3

Note: Respondents who indicated that they did not think they could easily access public benefits if needed were asked for the reasons behind this perceived difficulty. They were presented with five possible reasons and asked to tick all that they think apply. They could also choose "don't know".
Source: OECD Secretariat estimates based on OECD Risks that Matter survey (2020), https://www.oecd.org/social/risks-that-matter.htm.

3. Calls for greater social protection - if the price is right

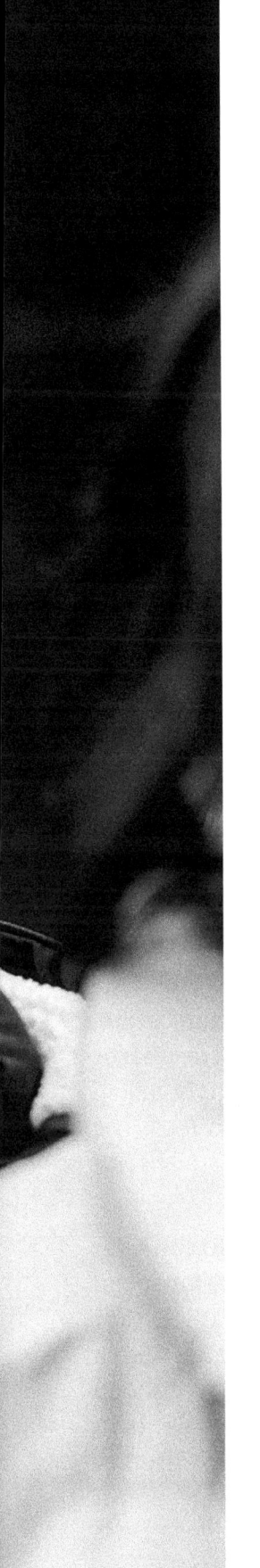

"The main challenge I have in the coming months is to keep my job. My company has already said it is not ruling out layoffs if the pandemic continues to affect people across the board. The government should help companies not lay off so many people. Although I realise that that is difficult."

– 46-year-old woman, Spain

The year 2020 was marked by high levels of anxiety – around personal health and economic security, prospects for the future, and concerns about the effectiveness of social protection in the face of a pandemic and an economic crisis.

OECD governments innovated quickly, expanded and enhanced coverage of social programmes, and implemented a battery of additional emergency measures to address serious threats to personal health and economic security in 2020. Nevertheless, many national, regional and local governments struggled to respond efficiently and thoroughly to save human lives and livelihoods. Issues like institutional capacity and inadequate funding sometimes hampered the effectiveness of COVID-19 social protection measures (OECD, 2021[1]).

As a result, despite unprecedented efforts in the provision of social protection, RTM 2020 reveals that many people are dissatisfied with their government's approach. Most would prefer a more expansive and higher quality safety net, even if they have to pay for it in the form of higher taxes. Most people are calling for higher taxes on the rich to help the poor. These results are in line with the results of RTM 2018, though attitudes have sharpened – especially among those who suffered economically due to COVID-19.

3.1. Support for a government safety net remains high throughout the OECD

The vast majority of respondents throughout the OECD call for either more spending to protect their economic and social security or for a continuation of current levels of spending. On average, 67.7% of all respondents say they think government should be doing more. Rates range from 41.2% in Denmark (where the social protection system is well-developed) to 92.9% in Chile. A majority of people in all but two countries —Denmark and Norway— say that government should be doing more. Perhaps unsurprisingly, in most countries, respondents whose household experienced job loss during COVID-19 were more likely to call for greater government intervention (Figure 3.1).

In countries where there is relatively lower support for additional social spending, it is worth noting that most of the rest of the respondents want those countries to continue to spend at the same level at which they currently do. 43.7% of respondents in Denmark, 27.3% in France, 35.95% in the Netherlands, 41.5% in Norway, and 34.4% in Switzerland say that they want government to spend about the same amount as they do now. France leads in the share of respondents who say they want government to spend less (15.3%), followed by Poland (12.2%), Turkey (11.6%) and the United States (11.3%).

On average across countries, women are 5 percentage points more likely than men to say that government should be doing more to ensure their economic and social security – perhaps reflecting the higher perceived economic risks many women cite.

3.2. Putting a price tag on social security

The delivery of social programmes comes at a cost to the government and to taxpayers, of course. The fiscal cost of social spending has not been at the forefront of policy discussions thus far, as generally OECD governments have recognised that they need to do "whatever it takes" to protect people and jobs during the crisis (OECD, 2020$_{[2]}$). Yet most governments are borrowing at unprecedented levels (at least in peacetime) to survive the crisis (OECD, 2020$_{[17]}$). Budgetary costs and hard decisions about which programmes and populations to prioritise will surely become more pressing political issues as governments move into the recovery period. RTM attempts to gauge the political feasibility of specific reforms by reminding respondents of the cost of social protection.

When respondents are primed to consider the tax and social contribution costs of specific expansions in the welfare state, support for government spending decreases relative to when people are simply asked whether government should do less, the same or more to ensure their security (Figure 3.1).

Nevertheless, even when asked to consider cost, a sizeable degree of support for social protection spending remains – at least for specific programmes. When primed with a fairly general reminder of the cost of social programmes, a majority of respondents in all 25 countries voice support for greater spending in at least one policy area, but typically more.

When considering the taxes they might have to pay and the benefits they might receive, seven out of ten respondents across countries say that they would support greater spending on public health services

Figure 3.1. Demands for greater government support are common, regardless of job security during the pandemic

Percent of respondents responding "more" or "much more" when asked "Do you think the government should be doing less, about the same, or more to ensure your economic and social security and well-being?", by reported experience of job loss in the household since the start of the pandemic, 2020

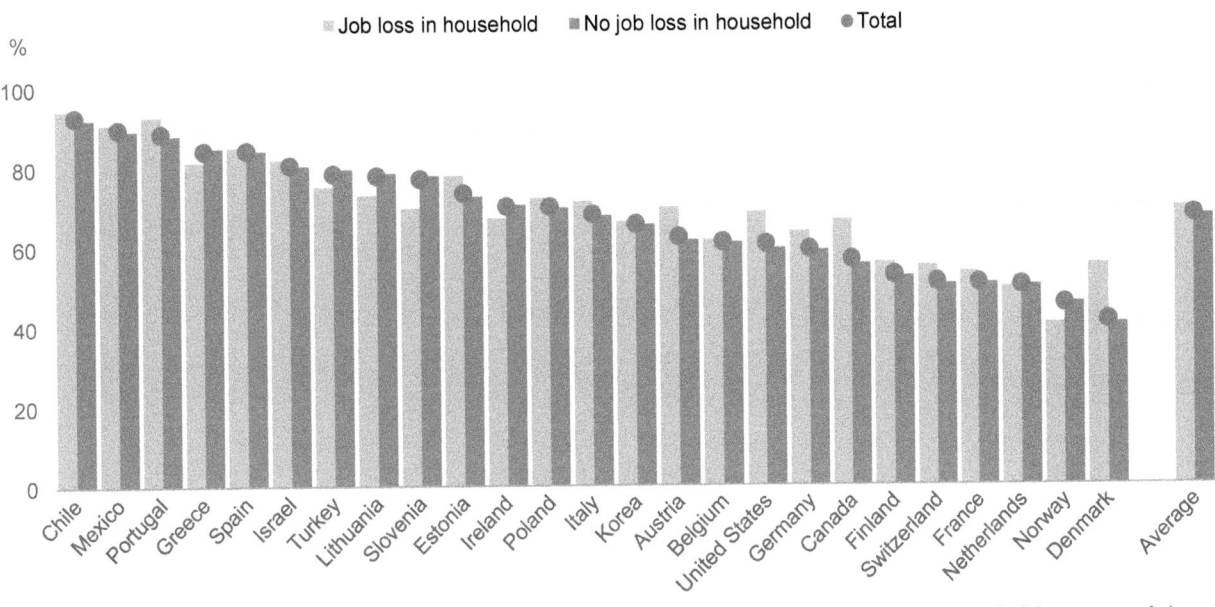

Note: Respondents were asked whether they thought the government should be doing less, more, or the same as they are currently doing to ensure their economic and social security. Possible response options were "much less", "less", "about the same as now", "more" and "much more". Respondents could also choose "don't know". "Job loss in household" refers to respondents reporting that either they or any member of their household have/has either "Lost their job or been laid off permanently by their employer" and/or "Lost their self-employed job or their own business", since the start of the COVID-19 pandemic.
Source: OECD Secretariat estimates based on the OECD Risks That Matter 2020 survey, https://www.oecd.org/social/risks-that-matter.htm

Figure 3.2. Women more likely to call on government to help ensure economic and social security

Percent of respondents responding "more" or "much more" when asked "Do you think the government should be doing less, about the same, or more to ensure your economic and social security and well-being?", by gender, 2020

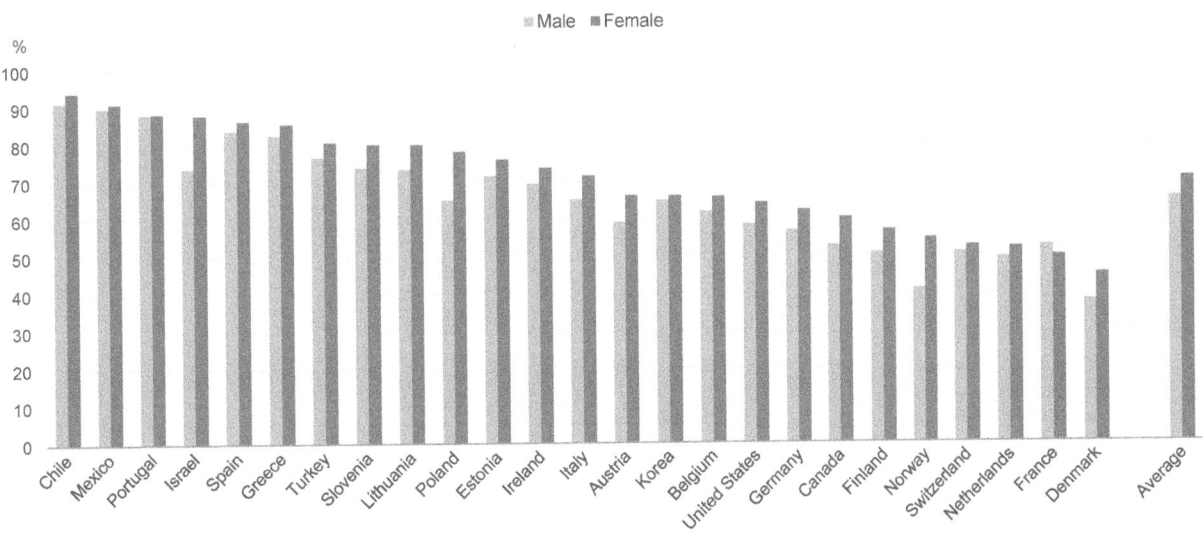

Note: Respondents were asked whether they thought the government should be doing less, more, or the same as they are currently doing to ensure their economic and social security. Possible response options were "much less", "less", "about the same as now", "more" and "much more". Respondents could also choose "don't know".
Source: OECD Secretariat estimates based on the OECD Risks That Matter 2020 survey, https://www.oecd.org/social/risks-that-matter.htm

3. Calls for greater social protection - if the price is right

Table 3.1. Nearly seven out of ten respondents say governments should spend more on health services when there is no specific cost in taxes

Percent of respondents indicating that they would like to see the government spend more or much more in the following policy areas, bearing in mind the taxes the respondent's household might have to pay and the benefits they might receive, 2020

	Family Support	Education	Employment Supports	Unemployment Supports	Income Supports	Housing Supports	Health Supports	Incapacity-related supports	Pensions	Long-term care	Public safety
Austria	46.6	56.7	46.7	33.5	45.2	48.3	67.8	60.3	66.8	74.1	45.6
Belgium	32.6	46.5	38.5	27.3	39.8	31.1	64.7	47.1	61.1	60.2	47.1
Canada	39.1	49.5	41.0	42.6	47.7	46.5	67.7	49.2	53.7	65.9	33.5
Chile	77.3	86.3	80.5	80.1	83.0	79.9	90.3	85.6	90.4	87.3	76.9
Denmark	23.0	38.0	27.5	28.2	24.5	18.3	57.8	34.7	44.1	61.3	49.1
Estonia	55.7	47.8	50.3	54.1	57.7	47.6	71.2	68.3	72.2	70.9	35.5
Finland	33.2	43.3	37.8	31.0	31.5	25.7	57.4	42.2	51.9	64.1	52.3
France	35.9	50.0	47.5	27.3	24.1	33.8	65.3	57.5	66.4	64.1	60.9
Germany	48.4	64.5	43.2	38.3	53.5	50.4	63.2	55.5	74.1	70.8	59.3
Greece	70.8	78.7	74.2	76.8	72.1	68.0	86.2	76.3	75.3	74.4	63.6
Ireland	47.5	62.5	52.6	34.6	44.6	52.8	78.5	64.6	62.5	74.5	59.3
Israel	64.0	72.3	69.7	68.9	64.3	66.5	80.0	72.5	72.4	77.8	62.2
Italy	64.4	72.1	72.5	63.6	61.0	55.4	76.2	68.0	69.7	72.6	68.1
Korea	43.3	34.9	46.4	39.9	41.0	47.2	52.4	53.2	41.1	47.4	48.3
Lithuania	60.3	61.3	62.8	59.7	65.5	57.5	68.9	68.9	79.3	73.8	48.5
Mexico	62.2	78.3	74.0	71.4	60.4	68.9	83.5	72.5	75.9	73.8	80.9
Netherlands	30.1	51.0	38.9	31.2	36.3	40.2	63.1	41.1	53.4	61.1	52.2
Norway	28.2	38.2	32.9	35.7	40.6	30.5	57.7	41.9	52.4	58.6	52.4
Poland	51.4	57.4	67.4	55.7	61.5	59.4	75.7	71.4	81.2	71.0	55.1
Portugal	71.5	72.4	67.1	59.9	35.6	56.8	85.9	80.2	72.0	81.3	66.7
Slovenia	55.3	51.2	57.2	49.8	51.8	61.2	72.1	70.9	78.4	77.7	33.5
Spain	56.9	75.0	66.4	61.1	54.4	59.0	82.4	71.7	70.7	78.3	52.0
Switzerland	45.6	47.5	47.3	39.5	45.8	43.4	51.6	49.8	64.6	55.9	33.1
Turkey	72.0	73.4	78.4	76.6	80.0	70.2	69.9	76.0	78.0	71.8	55.5
United States	49.0	53.0	50.2	48.3	50.1	46.2	59.3	50.5	42.8	55.4	49.0
Average	50.6	58.5	54.8	49.4	50.9	50.6	70.0	61.2	66.0	69.0	53.6

Note: Respondents were asked whether they would like to see less, the same, or more government spending in different social policy areas, given the taxes they might have to pay and the benefits they and their family might receive. Possible response options were "spend much less", "spend less", "spend the same as now", "spend more" and "spend much more". Respondents could also choose "can't choose". Table shows an aggregation of the results "spend more" and "spend much more" per country and issue area.
Source: OECD Secretariat estimates based on the OECD Risks That Matter 2020 survey, https://www.oecd.org/social/risks-that-matter.htm.

Figure 3.3. Health, pensions and long-term care are the spending priorities in most countries

Percent of respondents indicating that they would like to see the government spend more or much more in the following policy areas, sorted by highest priority issue in each country, bearing in mind the taxes the respondent's household might have to pay and the benefits they might receive, 2020

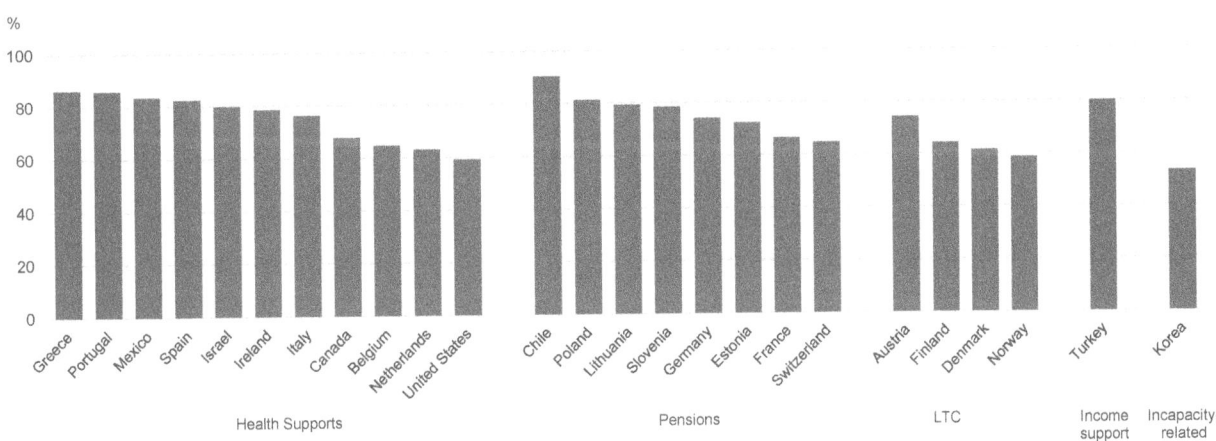

Note: Respondents were asked whether they would like to see less, the same, or more government spending in different social policy areas, given the taxes they might have to pay and the benefits they and their family might receive. Possible response options were "spend much less", "spend less", "spend the same as now", "spend more" and "spend much more". Respondents could also choose "none" or "can't choose". Figure presents the issue with the greatest share of respondents indicating willingness to pay, per country. The full list of responses was family supports, education services and supports, employment supports, unemployment supports, income supports, housing supports, health supports, incapacity-related supports, pensions, long-term services for the elderly, public safety, none, and don't know. Table shows an aggregation of the results "spend more" and "spend much more" per country and issue area.
Source: OECD Secretariat estimates based on the OECD Risks That Matter 2020 survey, https://www.oecd.org/social/risks-that-matter.htm.

Figure 3.4. Respondents experiencing job loss during the pandemic are more likely to call for government action on pocketbook issues

Percent of respondents reporting that they would like government to spend "more" or "much more" on each policy area, by reported experience of job loss in the household since the start of the COVID-19 pandemic, unweighted cross-country average, 2020

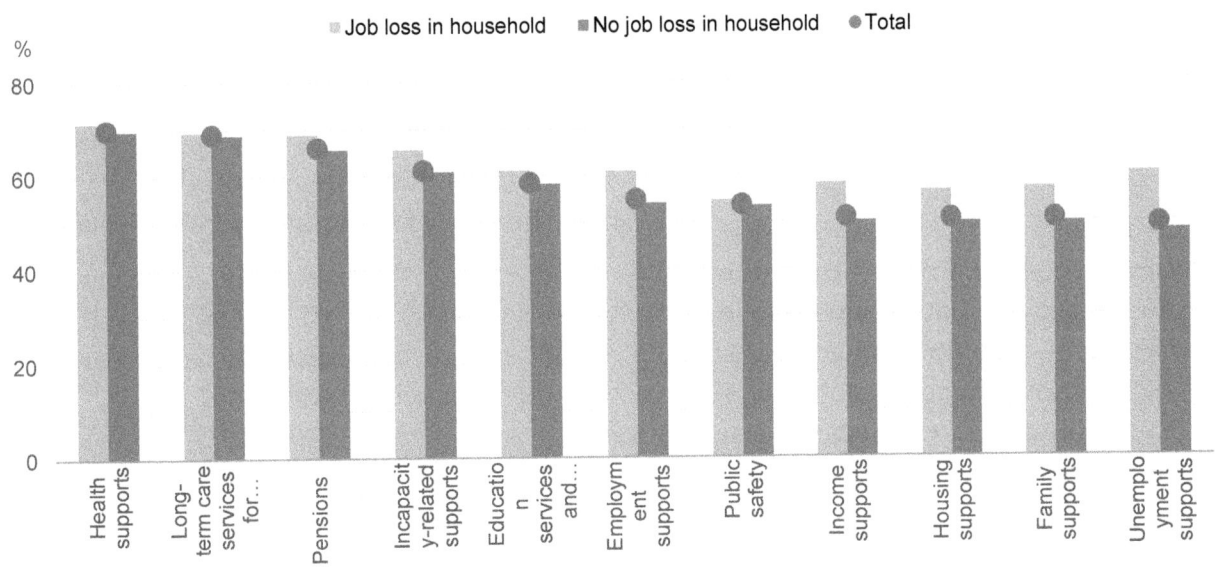

Note: Respondents were asked whether they would like to see less, the same, or more government spending in different social policy areas, given the taxes they might have to pay and the benefits they and their family might receive. Possible response options were "spend much less", "spend less", "spend the same as now", "spend more" and "spend much more". Respondents could also choose "can't choose". "Job loss in household" refers to respondents reporting that either they or any member of their household have/has either "Lost their job or been laid off permanently by their employer" and/or "Lost their self-employed job or their own business", since the start of the COVID-19 pandemic.
Source: OECD Secretariat estimates based on the OECD Risks That Matter 2020 survey, https://www.oecd.org/social/risks-that-matter.htm.

– the most popular issue area (Table 3.1). Health services are also the top spending priority in 12 of the 25 countries surveyed in RTM 2020 (Figure 3.3).

There are many potential drivers of this result showing respondents' view of health services. The presence of a global pandemic surely encourages greater prioritisation of health care provision, though health was also a top perceived risk in RTM 2018 – it is a risk everyone shares. The desire for greater health care spending may also be related to the aforementioned result that people are most satisfied with health care provision – suggesting that people may be more willing to invest in services that they feel are provided (relatively) well.[7]

Perhaps related to their economic insecurity, respondents whose households lost jobs during COVID show a stronger willingness to pay more in taxes to receive better social protection. There is especially strong support in this group for better investments in employment supports (e.g. job search services, skills training, access to entrepreneurial funds), unemployment supports, and income supports like minimum income benefits (OECD, 2021[1]).

Across countries, 60.3% of respondents whose household experienced job loss say that – thinking about the taxes they might have to pay and the benefits they might receive – they would like the government to spend more or much more in order to provide better unemployment supports (e.g. unemployment benefits). This figure stands in contrast to the 48.1% of respondents who did not experience outright job loss during COVID who call for greater government spending on unemployment supports – though this is, of course, still a large share. In Austria, Canada, Finland, Slovenia, and the United States, the preference gap between people whose households lost jobs and those who did not is greater than 20 percentage points. This is a sizeable divergence in preferences following COVID insecurity.

The next set of questions put a price tag on social programmes: an additional 2% of income in taxes and social contributions. People are most willing to pay more for better provision of health care, again, but faced with the 2% figure, the share supporting spending more in this policy area drops to 44.7%, on average, across countries (Table 3.2) – down from 70% when the cost is described more generally (Table 3.1).

Pensions are the issue where respondents are second-most likely to support paying an additional 2% of income in taxes and social contributions, on average across countries (Figure 3.5). This could of course be related to the personalised nature of pension contributions, as many countries have links between lifetime contributions and individual benefits received in retirement. Using the "2% of income" definition of cost, support for pensions is greatest in Slovenia: 62.7% of respondents there say they would favour spending more on pensions, even at the cost of an additional 2% of income.

Importantly, this specific price tag proposes the same rate to all respondents; it does not account for redistributive preferences in terms of who should pay.

> "If I am unemployed [after college], I would need to rely on a different source for my basic needs, as my parents expect me to not rely on them after graduating. To address this, I hope the government can provide better resources for those who are unemployed, not just for sustenance, but also so they can find a job and escape that difficult financial situation."
>
> – 20-year-old-woman, the United States

3. Calls for greater social protection - if the price is right

Figure 3.5. Healthcare and pensions remain top issues when cost is mentioned, but support drops with a specific price tag

Percent of respondents responding selecting the top-rated policy area in each country when asked "Would you be willing to pay an additional 2% of your income in taxes and social contributions to benefit from better provision of and access to [insert policy area]", 2020

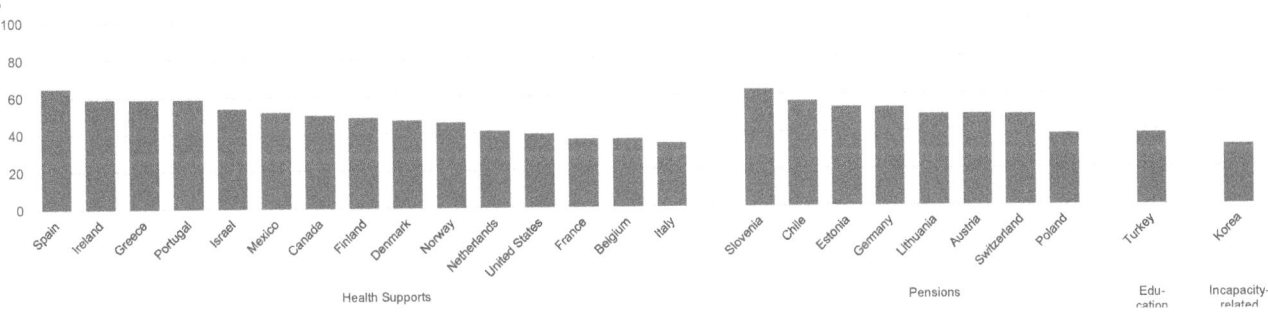

Note: Respondents were asked how willing they would be to pay an additional 2% of their income in taxes/social contributions to benefit from better provision of and access to a list of 11 supports. Possible response options were "spend much less", "spend less", "spend the same as now", "spend more" and "spend much more". Respondents could also choose "none" or "don't know" as a response option. Figure presents the issue with the greatest share of respondents indicating willingness to pay, per country, and the percentage willing to pay an additional 2% of their income in this area. (Top issues were health supports, pensions, education, or incapacity-related supports). The full list of responses was family supports, education services and supports, employment supports, unemployment supports, income supports, housing supports, health supports, incapacity-related supports, pensions, long-term services for the elderly, public safety, none, and don't know.
Source: OECD Secretariat estimates based on the OECD Risks That Matter 2020 survey, https://www.oecd.org/social/risks-that-matter.htm.

Figure 3.6. Most respondents would like government to do more to reduce income differences

Percent of respondents responding "more" or "much more" when asked "Governments can reduce income differences between the rich and the poor by collecting taxes and providing social benefits. In your country, do you think the government should do more or less to reduce income differences?", 2020

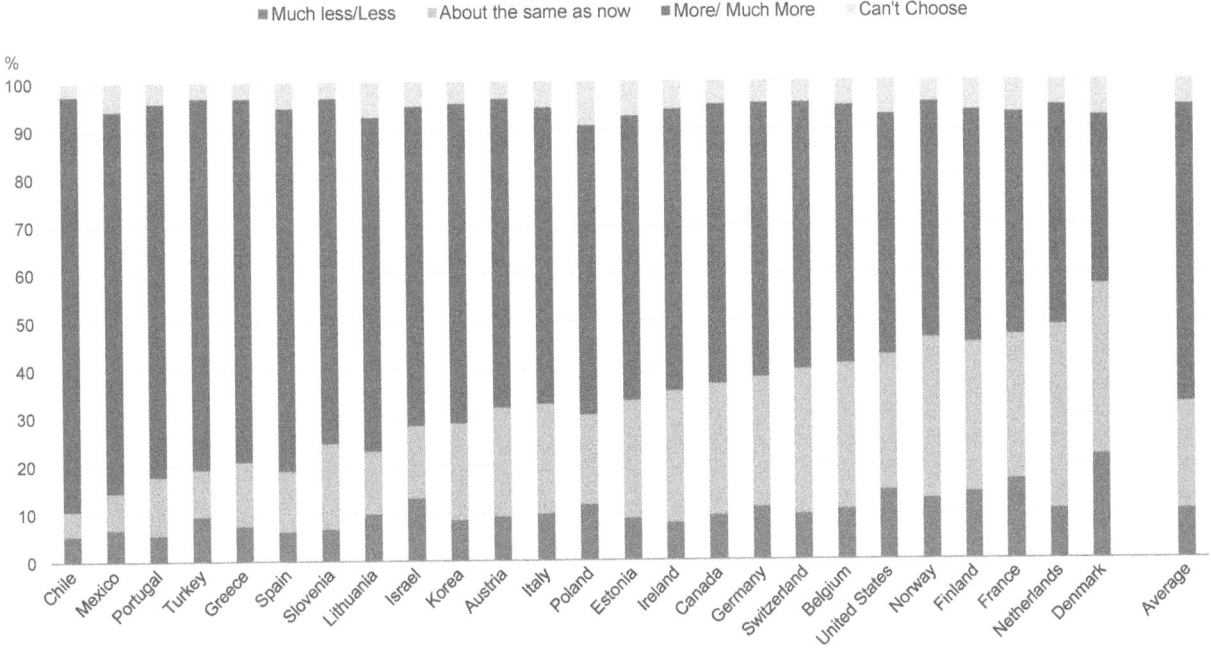

Note: Respondents were asked whether they thought the government should be doing less, more, or the same as they are currently doing to reduce income differences between the rich and the poor. Possible response options were "much less", "less", "about the same as now", "more" and "much more". Respondents could also choose "can't choose".
Source: OECD Secretariat estimates based on the OECD Risks That Matter 2020 survey, https://www.oecd.org/social/risks-that-matter.htm.

3.3. How to fund social programmes? Redistributive preferences in a pandemic

Much of the discussion thus far has focused on what might be considered the social insurance function of the welfare state – health care, pensions, unemployment insurance and so on, which provide people with a degree of support at specific moments in the life cycle.

When thinking about the redistributive function governments play in reducing income inequality, respondents across countries are generally supportive of government intervention. On average across countries, 62.2% of people say that government should do more, or much more, to reduce income differences between the rich and the poor by collecting taxes and providing social benefits (Figure 3.6).

The countries where people are least likely to call for more redistribution – Denmark, the Netherlands, France – tend to have already relatively high levels of redistribution. These countries also have relatively high levels of satisfaction with current redistributive measures. Across countries, very few people say that government should be doing less to reduce income differences. The cross-national average calling for less intervention to reduce inequality is 10.3%.

When asked specifically whether government should tax the rich more than they currently do in order to support the poor, 64.5% of respondents, on average across countries, reply "yes" or "definitely yes". This is slightly lower than the cross-national average in 2018, but since 2018 the rate also increased more in countries that are more unequal (OECD, 2021[18]). There is a slight positive correlation between the degree of income inequality in a country, measured by Gini, and demands for more redistribution and more progressive taxation (Figure 3.7) – suggesting that people are responding to inequality with demands for more redistribution. There is also a positive association between experiencing financial hardship during the pandemic and calls for greater redistribution (OECD, 2021[18]), similar to the findings looking at preferences for spending on specific programmes (Figure 3.4).

Figure 3.7. Higher inequality corresponds with greater calls for redistribution

Share of respondents who answer "more" or "much more" when asked whether government should redistribute more or tax the rich more, relative to Gini index of disposable income

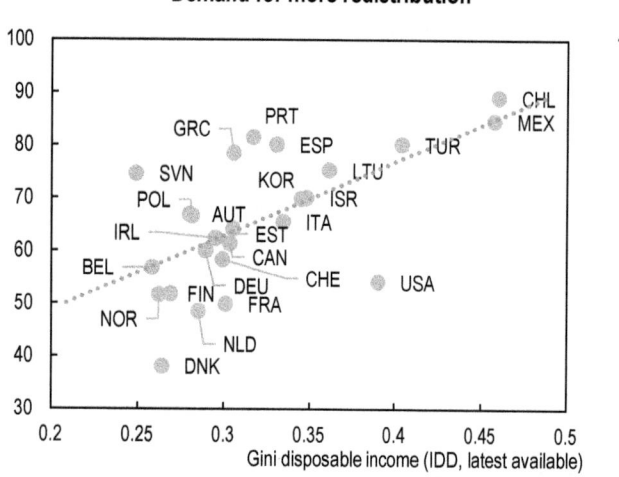
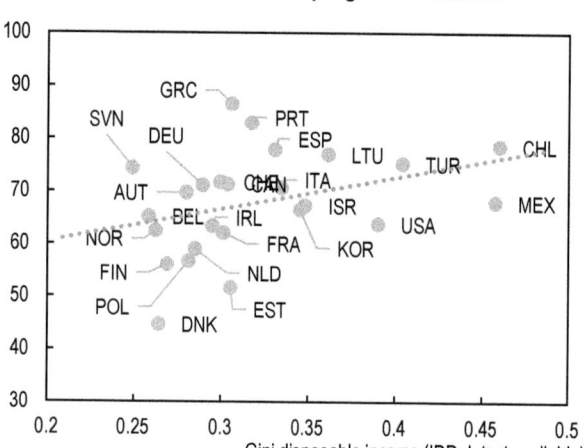

Note: The Gini disposable income refers to 2018, apart from Chile, Denmark, Germany, Ireland, Italy, Switzerland, USA (2017), Mexico, the Netherlands (2016), and Turkey (2015).
Source: OECD Secretariat estimates based on the OECD Income Distribution Database and the OECD Risks That Matter 2020 survey https://www.oecd.org/social/risks-that-matter.htm. Publication forthcoming in (OECD, 2021[18]).

> "In Mexico, no [political] party has done enough to reduce the gap between the rich and the poor. There have been some attempts, like a very low pension for seniors, but they are very low amounts."
>
> – 59-year-old man, Mexico

Table 3.2. Support for social spending decreases when there is a specific price tag

Percent of respondents responding selecting "yes" when asked whether they would be willing to pay an additional 2% of their income in taxes and social contributions to benefit from better provision of and access to each of the following policy areas, 2020

	Family Support	Education	Employment Supports	Unemployment Supports	Income Supports	Housing Supports	Health Supports	Incapacity-related supports	Pensions	Long-term care	Public safety	None
Austria	24,2	27,9	15,7	21,4	20,4	22,2	40,8	31,1	48,6	39,5	20,5	18,9
Belgium	13,8	18,5	10,9	10,7	15,4	9,6	36,5	21,3	36,3	27,0	20,0	24,0
Canada	23,4	29,3	21,4	23,8	27,6	25,4	49,9	25,0	39,3	35,6	18,1	15,8
Chile	27,4	39,2	28,8	37,0	30,8	38,4	54,9	32,0	56,2	38,5	27,6	14,1
Denmark	13,6	22,1	13,8	15,7	11,1	12,0	46,9	22,9	33,6	39,5	31,0	18,3
Estonia	35,2	24,9	22,2	34,6	28,1	21,5	45,3	40,1	52,8	37,1	13,9	11,1
Finland	21,1	29,2	19,0	21,0	18,7	14,9	48,5	24,0	37,5	40,8	35,1	13,9
France	14,0	17,4	14,4	11,0	8,3	12,8	36,5	23,1	36,2	27,3	25,6	25,8
Germany	24,2	29,1	12,6	20,2	21,0	22,6	35,8	28,6	52,4	35,8	28,8	16,5
Greece	36,8	39,7	31,9	42,0	35,4	29,1	58,8	34,4	45,4	32,3	30,3	15,8
Ireland	29,3	40,2	22,9	19,7	21,6	29,9	59,0	35,1	47,5	43,2	33,8	12,1
Israel	34,1	39,5	27,0	34,8	31,0	33,9	53,7	33,1	38,2	42,4	27,1	16,6
Italy	19,3	20,8	18,9	18,3	17,1	10,0	34,1	16,9	24,3	19,5	19,8	21,8
Korea	19,7	13,8	17,3	22,5	22,8	24,3	30,8	31,7	28,2	24,1	20,4	10,4
Lithuania	29,8	23,1	22,3	32,6	22,5	21,6	32,0	32,9	48,7	30,4	12,5	8,8
Mexico	23,0	38,1	33,7	36,6	21,5	36,3	51,6	31,9	47,7	32,9	41,2	13,5
Netherlands	13,9	21,8	11,4	13,5	14,5	14,3	41,1	16,2	32,8	27,6	21,9	21,3
Norway	21,5	21,8	13,9	19,5	20,3	17,1	45,8	29,4	40,7	36,3	27,2	13,9
Poland	18,9	20,6	21,7	15,3	19,3	19,9	33,2	29,5	37,9	24,8	15,2	18,3
Portugal	35,5	34,6	27,8	30,6	12,3	25,3	58,8	39,5	41,9	44,4	30,3	13,6
Slovenia	33,7	27,2	26,7	40,3	30,7	35,1	55,7	48,1	62,7	51,6	14,8	10,5
Spain	30,8	45,4	34,4	38,3	31,2	34,6	64,8	42,6	57,0	44,0	25,4	11,7
Switzerland	25,7	23,7	21,1	25,1	27,2	20,8	31,3	29,0	48,3	33,0	19,1	15,8
Turkey	26,4	38,1	28,1	35,6	31,8	26,2	31,9	26,8	34,3	27,3	16,4	11,4
United States	25,1	28,7	23,0	23,9	25,8	22,7	39,3	21,7	18,8	26,0	23,7	17,6
Average	24,8	28,6	21,6	25,8	22,7	23,2	44,7	29,9	41,9	34,4	24,0	15,7

Note: Respondents were asked whether they would like to see less, the same, or more government spending in different social policy areas, given the taxes they might have to pay and the benefits they and their family might receive. Possible response options were "spend much less", "spend less", "spend the same as now", "spend more" and "spend much more". Respondents could also choose "can't choose". Table shows an aggregation of the results "spend more" and "spend much more" per country and issue area.
Source: OECD Secretariat estimates based on the OECD Risks That Matter 2020 survey, https://www.oecd.org/social/risks-that-matter.htm.

References

Barone, G. and S. Mocetti (2011), "Tax morale and public spending inefficiency", International Tax and Public Finance, Vol. 18/6, pp. 724 749, http://dx.doi.org/10.1007/s10797 011 9174 z. [19]

Carman, K. and S. Nataraj (2020), How Are Americans Paying Their Bills During the COVID-19 Pandemic?, RAND Corporation, http://dx.doi.org/10.7249/rra308 3. [13]

European Parliament / Eurobarometer (2020), Uncertainty/EU/Hope: Public Opinion in the Times of COVID-19, European Parliament, Brussels, https://www.europarl.europa.eu/at-your-service/en/be heard/eurobarometer/public-opinion-in-the eu in-time of-coronavirus-crisis (accessed on 24 February 2021). [12]

Feld, L. and B. Frey (2002), "Deterrence and Morale in Taxation: An Empirical Analysis", CESinfo Working Paper Series, Vol. 760, https://ideas.repec.org/p/ces/ceswps/_760.html (accessed on 6 April 2021). [20]

Gentilini, U. et al. (2021), Social Protection and Jobs Responses to COVID 19: A Real-Time Review of Country Measures, World Bank, Washington, DC., https://openknowledge.worldbank.org/handle/10986/33635 (accessed on 6 April 2021). [15]

ISSA (2021), Coronavirus country measures | International Social Security Association (ISSA), https://ww1.issa.int/coronavirus/country-measures (accessed on 25 March 2021). [7]

OECD (2021), Building for a better tomorrow: Policies to make housing more affordable, OECD Publishing, Paris, https://read.oecd-ilibrary.org/view/?ref=1060_10600750ejk3l4uil&title=ENG_OECD-affordable housing-policies-brief (accessed on 29 March 2021). [14]

OECD (2021), COVID-19 and Long-Term Care: Impact, Policy Responses and the Way Forward, OECD Publishing, Paris. [9]

OECD (2021), OECD Economic Outlook, Volume 2021 Issue 1, OECD Publishing, Paris, https://dx.doi.org/10.1787/edfbca02 en. [22]

OECD (2021), OECD Employment Outlook 2021, OECD Publishing, Paris, https://doi.org/10.1787/5a700c4b-en. [3]

OECD (2021), Perceptions of inequality and preferences for redistribution, OECD Publishing, Paris. [18]

OECD (2021), Risks that Matter 2020: The long reach of COVID-19, OECD Publishing, Paris, https://www.oecd.org/social/risks-that-matter.htm (accessed on 22 June 2021). [1]

OECD (2021), Short-Term Labour Market Statistics, https://stats.oecd.org/index.aspx?queryid=35253 (accessed on 25 March 2021). [8]

OECD (2021), Young people's concerns during COVID 19: Results from Risks that Matter 2020, https://doi.org/10.1787/64b51763 en. [11]

OECD (2020), Job retention schemes during the COVID-19 lockdown and beyond, OECD Publishing, Paris, http://www.oecd.org/coronavirus/policy-responses/job-retention-schemes-during-the-COVID-19 lockdown-and-beyond 0853ba1d/ (accessed on 29 January 2021). [4]

OECD (2020), OECD Data: Elderly population, OECD Publishing, Paris, https://data.oecd.org/pop/elderly-population.htm. [10]

OECD (2020), OECD Employment Outlook 2020: Worker Security and the COVID 19 Crisis, OECD Publishing, Paris, https://dx.doi.org/10.1787/1686c758 en. [2]

OECD (2020), Social partnership in the times of the COVID-19 pandemic – OECD, OECD Publishing, Paris, https://read.oecd-ilibrary.org/view/?ref=129_129652 rqw593axrl&title=Social-partnership-in-the-times-of-the COVID-19 pandemic (accessed on 29 January 2021). [5]

OECD (2020), Sovereign Borrowing Outlook 2020: Special COVID-19 edition, OECD Publishing, Paris, http://dx.doi.org/10.1787/9789264298828 en. [17]

OECD (2020), Supporting livelihoods during the COVID-19 crisis: Closing the gaps in safety nets, OECD Publishing, Paris, http://www.oecd.org/coronavirus/policy-responses/supporting-livelihoods-during-the COVID -9 crisis-closing-the gaps-in-safety-nets 17cbb92d/ (accessed on 29 January 2021). [6]

OECD (2019), Risks that Matter: Main Findings from the 2018 OECD Risks That Matter Survey, OECD Publishing, Paris, http://www.oecd.org/social/risks-that-matter.htm (accessed on 2 April 2020). [16]

Ortega, D. et al. (2016), "Reciprocity and Willingness to Pay Taxes: Evidence from a Survey Experiment in Latin America", Economía Journal, Vol. Volume 16 Number 2/Spring 2016, pp. 55 87, https://EconPapers.repec.org/RePEc: col:000425:014 410 (accessed on 6 April 2021). [21]

Annex A. Occurrence of financial difficulties during COVID-19

Annex Table 1. Nearly one-third of households in OECD had trouble paying bills during COVID 19

Percent of respondents reporting each of the following financial difficulties since the start of the COVID-19 pandemic, 2020

	Failed to pay a usual expense	Taken money out of own savings or sold assets	Taken money from friends or extended family	Taken on additional debt or used credit	Asked a charity or non-profit institution for assistance	Gone hungry because could not afford food	Lost your home as could not afford the mortgage or rent	Declared bankruptcy or asked bank for assistance	Any of the above
Austria	4.2	15.9	5.2	2.3	1.7	1.1	0.6	0.7	22.5
Belgium	4.2	11.0	5.3	2.6	1.4	3.0	1.4	1.3	20.2
Canada	8.8	20.8	6.6	12.5	2.7	4.1	0.8	0.7	32.3
Chile	28.6	42.6	18.7	16.3	6.7	6.8	1.4	2.5	61.2
Denmark	1.4	9.3	5.0	3.9	1.2	2.3	1.0	0.6	17.4
Estonia	7.1	17.9	9.1	7.9	2.2	4.6	2.1	0.9	30.6
Finland	6.9	13.6	5.6	4.2	1.6	1.6	0.5	0.7	21.6
France	6.5	10.3	4.6	3.3	1.5	2.9	0.6	0.4	21.0
Germany	3.9	12.2	5.1	3.3	1.6	2.0	0.4	0.9	18.7
Greece	27.5	20.1	16.3	2.4	2.0	13.8	1.3	0.4	48.9
Ireland	9.6	20.4	7.8	8.0	1.5	2.2	0.9	0.8	30.7
Israel	8.3	18.2	9.2	9.7	2.9	2.1	0.8	0.2	29.9
Italy	9.7	16.9	6.0	5.5	3.4	1.7	1.4	0.4	29.6
Korea	4.0	6.8	5.8	6.7	1.8	2.4	1.1	0.7	19.0
Lithuania	6.4	14.4	8.2	3.5	2.3	2.8	1.6	0.5	25.7
Mexico	26.4	40.1	27.0	18.7	7.0	10.7	1.3	2.2	66.1
Netherlands	3.3	9.0	3.8	2.4	2.2	2.0	0.5	1.1	15.6
Norway	5.2	13.0	7.2	4.0	2.6	3.8	1.5	0.6	23.2
Poland	12.1	10.3	9.8	8.1	3.4	7.3	1.9	1.1	32.9
Portugal	7.0	17.0	5.7	5.2	2.1	1.9	0.4	0.6	25.5
Slovenia	12.9	23.4	9.0	7.1	3.7	2.8	0.8	1.1	34.2
Spain	6.7	18.9	5.6	4.4	2.0	1.6	0.3	0.6	27.4
Switzerland	6.8	14.5	7.0	3.5	3.0	3.2	1.2	0.8	25.4
Turkey	28.5	28.5	22.2	23.8	9.3	6.2	5.3	3.4	61.2
United States	12.2	20.2	10.8	12.7	5.8	5.6	2.5	1.1	33.7
Average	10.3	17.8	9.1	7.3	3.0	3.9	1.3	1.0	31.0

Note: Respondents were asked whether, at any time since the start of the COVID 19 pandemic, they (or their household) had experienced one or more of a range of specific finance related events, listed in the above columns. Respondents could select all the options that applied.
Source: OECD Secretariat estimates based on the OECD Risks That Matter 2020 survey, https://www.oecd.org/social/risks-that-matter.htm.

Notes

1. This 7% figure holds across ten countries for which up-to-date labour force statistics on work hours are available (Australia, Canada, Chile, Iceland, Japan, Korea, Mexico, Sweden, the United Kingdom, and the United States), as well as for the OECD as a whole, using figures from quarterly national accounts in countries for which labour force survey data for Q1 2021 are not yet available.

2. This popular confidence is not misplaced: Lithuania is projected to have one of the fastest returns to pre-pandemic per capita GDP (OECD, 2021[22]).

3. Respondents with neither partner employed at the time of the interview are excluded from this estimate.

4. This was intended to prevent an over-representation of 65- to 70-year-olds within the sample of non-employed people (and therefore an under-representation of working age non-employed people).

5. These findings are detailed further in the report "The Long Reach of COVID-19" (OECD, 2021[1]).

6. This is the net mandatory and voluntary pension replacement rate, as percent of pre-retirement earnings for male earner at 100% of average wage entering the labour market today

7. Some of the tax morale literature supports this idea, finding that effective public programmes and interactions with competent and respectful public authorities help drive tax compliance. Seminal works include (Barone and Mocetti, 2011[19]) and (Feld and Frey, 2002[20]). More recent experimental literature has also found positive relationships between the quality of public services and willingness to pay taxes (see for example (Ortega et al., 2016[21]).

Contacts:

Monika Queisser (monika.queisser@oecd.org),
Valerie Frey (valerie.frey@oecd.org),
OECD Directorate for Employment, Labour, and Social Affairs

@OECD_Social

www.oecd.org/social/risks-that-matter.htm

Image credits:

Cover Page: © Shutterstock/Artem Oleshko
Pages 2-3: © Shutterstock/Tomsickova Tatyana
Pages 4-5: © Shutterstock/Alpha Lyrae
Pages 8-9: Shutterstock/Vladislav Gajic
Page 10: Shutterstock/insta_photos
Page 12-13: © Shutterstock/Zoran Zeremski
Pages 26-27: © Shutterstock/CGN_089
Pages 28-29: Shutterstock/Iryna Inshyna
Page 40-41: © Shutterstock/Volurol
Page 52-53: © Shutterstock/Krakenimages.com

www.ingramcontent.com/pod-product-compliance
Ingram Content Group UK Ltd.
Pitfield, Milton Keynes, MK11 3LW, UK
UKHW051300180426
11947UKWH00020B/1813